M000233951

In his book, *What the Bible Says About I*
biblical account of the creation and
present, and future. The volume pro
stretching from the early chapters of Genesis and throughout the rest of the Bible.
Pastor McManis also speaks to current events that are informed by God's
revelation about Israel and gives practical suggestions about how a Christian
should respond to Israel. I am confident that this work will serve the church well
in helping individuals and congregations think about and appreciate the important
role that Israel has played and will play in God's plans.

Randall L. McKinion, Ph.D.
Assistant Vice President for Academic Affairs
Professor of Old Testament, *Cedarville University*, Cedarville, OH

In the last two decades there has been a rise of different forms of Replacement
Theology and with it a surge of theological anti-semitism which requires an
ignoring of the plain meaning of the text and leads to imaginative allegorical
interpretations. The result is the claim that what the biblical text states is not what
it means and what it means is what the expositor says it means. Cliff McManis has
written an easy to read but also a comprehensive study of what the Scriptures
really teach about Israel: past, present, and future and at the same time provides a
very good critique of the fallacy of Replacement Theology.

Arnold Fruchtenbaum, Ph.D.
Author of *Israelology: The Missing Link in Systematic Theology*
Ariel Ministries, San Antonio, TX

Pastor McManis provides a solid overview of God's promises to and intentions
for His chosen people, Israel. He also gives attention to more modern issues and
misunderstandings related to Israel. He starts where everyone should, with the
creation week and God's intentions for the world. He then develops the
covenantal foundation for all Scripture that also reveals Israel's role in God's plan
for His created world. Unlike much of the scholarly world that either disregards
the OT revelation concerning God's plan for Israel or reinterprets it, McManis
shows that the NT builds on the OT message, looking forward to God
establishing His kingdom over the entire earth, anchored in the land of promise
where the redeemed nation of Israel has been reinstalled. This volume deserves
reading by God's people who are interested in handling God's Word well.

Michael A. Grisanti, Ph.D.
Chair of Old Testament Department, Director of TMS Israel Study Trip
Distinguished Research Professor of Old Testament
The Master's Seminary, Sun Valley, CA

There is no more important nation in the world than Israel. If you want to observe what God is doing and will do in the world, watch Israel because this nation is God's covenant people. It is true that the nation is quite secular today as are all other nations, but Israel is still the people of God and God will take care of His people. Dr. McManis has done a masterful job in giving the reader a historical understanding of this precious nation as well as what God will do with the nation in the future. He is to be commended for his biblical and theological accuracy from the very foundation of the earth in Genesis 1 to the Millennial Kingdom and eternal state in Revelation 22. I am convinced that you will learn much and be encouraged in what God's future is for Israel and for humanity. Enjoy the book!

Thomas A. Halstead, Ed.D.
Dean, School of Biblical Studies, *The Master's University*, Santa Clarita, CA

The topic of Israel is a political and theological issue today and has been so for thousands of years. Politically, loud voices are insisting that Israel has no right to her land. Theologically, many Christians have been taught that the Christian church has permanently replaced Israel in God's plan for the future. If you are looking for solid biblical responses to these unbiblical ideas, this is the book for you. *What the Bible Says about Israel* is true to its title, explaining clearly and carefully from the Scriptures why Israel does have a right to her land, and why Israel is indeed a central player in God's plan for the future. And there is other related information in the book that all Christians should know such as the historical derivation of the word, "Palestine." I recommend that you read this book. It will be a spiritual encouragement to you to learn more about the faithfulness of God to Israel—and to you.

Larry Pettegrew, Th.D.
General editor of *Forsaking Israel: How it Happened & Why it Matters*
Research Professor of Theology, *Shepherds Theological Seminary*, Cary, NC

Israel takes center stage in the Bible and in world affairs. In this light Cliff McManis is a true "centrist." He knows what the Bible is about and he knows that it is about Israel. He knows about history (both ancient and modern) and knows it has had and has its focus on Israel. He also knows about prophecy (gratefully from a consistent literal futurist interpretation) and knows it is also about Israel. He is to be congratulated for writing a book anyone can read—and should read—to set the record straight and to set their compass on Israel's great hope in Messiah's coming and His Kingdom.

J. Randall Price, Ph.D.
Author of *What Should We Think About Israel?*
President, World of the Bible Ministries;
Co-director of the Qumran Cave Excavation;
Distinguished Research Professor of Biblical & Judaic Studies, *Liberty University*, Lynchburg, Virginia; Curator – Liberty Biblical Museum

Far too often Christians find themselves being overwhelmed by an avalanche of resources intent upon denying the Scripture's description of Israel as God's chosen people. Some look at biblical Israel as nothing more than some sort of spiritual allegory. Others, choking on the toxic fumes of secular humanism, question the authority of Scripture to begin with. Amazingly, in the midst of an era of so-called "political correctness," many Christians and non-Christians alike strip "true Israel" of any future identity. Why does such anti-semitism show its ugly face even within the church? The Bible answers that question—and many others. McManis mines the Bible's historical, prophetic, and theological teachings in both testaments to identify Israel past, present, and future. God's covenant with Abraham unlocks the vast body of truth about Israel within the pages of Scripture. Grab your Bible. Sit down to read McManis' *What the Bible Says about Israel*. It's time to free your theological compass of the magnetic distractions of covenantalism, anti-semitism, and the scoffers who mock the clear teaching of God's authoritative and inerrant Word.

William D. Barrick, Ph.D.

Emeritus Professor of Old Testament, *The Master's Seminary*;
Chairman, Board of Directors, Canyon Ministries;
Old Testament Editor, *Evangelical Exegetical Commentary*

The
EQUIP
Series

What the Bible Says About
Israel
Past, Present & Future

Cliff McManis

With All Wisdom
Cupertino, CA

What the Bible Says About
Israel
Past, Present & Future

Affectionately dedicated to the memory of
Ruth "with the truth" Wardell;
Woman of God;
Lover of Jews;
Relentless evangelist;
Christ-like example to all.

Contents

Acknowledgments

I want to thank the many saints who helped bring this book to its final form. First, thanks to the dear saints of Creekside Bible Church who allow me the privilege of being the Pastor-teacher in their local fellowship where I have the opportunity to fulfill "the ministry of the Word" (Acts 6:2) on a regular basis by preaching and teaching the Bible. Like the Bereans of Paul's day, they are noble-minded and welcome the Word with great eagerness and discernment (Acts 17:10-11). They were enthusiastic and edified when I preached a series of four sermons a few years ago on "What the Bible Says about Israel." That sermon series was expanded in written form and became the current volume. I also want to thank the Elders of Creekside: Derek Brown, J. R. Cuevas, Bob Douglas, Justin Duran, Sam Kim, Peter Lam, and Tim Wong. Thanks for being faithful shepherds of the local church and for being incredibly supportive of me in the written task of the ministry of the Word on behalf of the saints. You brothers are a sheer joy to minister with.

Thanks to the whole With All Wisdom (WAW) Publications team who were a tremendous blessing to me throughout the whole project—to the editors: Jasmine Patton, J. R. Cuevas and Austin Thompson; the proof-readers: Tim Anderson and John Platz; the whole WAW design team and especially Oluwasanya Awe (aka, the Big "O"), for layout and design of the cover as well as the daunting and unmatched task of composing the fifteen maps of Israel in the Appendix and Melissa Kim for labeling the maps. Thanks to the associate editor of WAW, Breanna Lynn (McManis) Paniagua, for molding the manuscript from beginning to end over a two-year period to bring it to fruition. And thanks to the managing editor of With All Wisdom Publications, Derek Brown, for overseeing the entire process with excellence, making it all even possible.

A special thanks to the amazing, long-time Old Testament Bible teachers and scholars who took time out of their demanding schedules to review the pre-publication manuscript and submit personal endorsements for the book. These men have proved themselves faithful for years, even decades, when it comes to teaching God's people the proper biblical perspective regarding Israel. My theology, ecclesiology and eschatology has been shaped over the years by their teaching: Dr. Bill Barrick, Dr. Arnold Fruchtenbaum, Dr. Michael Grisanti, Dr. Tom Halstead, Dr. Randy McKinion, Dr. Larry Pettegrew and Dr. Randy Price.

Introduction

Israel. What comes to your mind when you hear that word? When you hear that name? It actually ranks as one of the most volatile names today—reactions to it range across the spectrum. Some would say Israel is God's special nation. Others say Israel was God's nation, but it is now wayward for the time. Some Christians say Israel has no special place in God's program today or in the future. Other people have utter contempt for Israel, and all Jews, accusing them of being violent oppressors, manipulative money-grubbers and a menace to the human race. All the disparate perspectives can actually be seen on any given day in various news outlets and websites. All views are current, at odds and stoking up emotion in every quarter.

In America today Israel is a flashpoint of controversy more than ever. The topic of Israel now divides political parties and is a main talking point for political candidates running for office. Prospective candidates need to have honed politically correct views on Israel right alongside their positions on abortion, healthcare, immigration, the environment and the economy. That hasn't always been the case. Up until just recently, say around 2008, America has always been an outspoken ally and advocate for Israel and the Jews. Not anymore. Time changes everything. For the first time ever, America has elected political officials who are overtly anti-

Semitic and who grow more caustic in their disdain for the Jew, and the nation of Israel, as the days go by.

Just go to the local American public college campus for proof. There is no topic that exudes greater overt politically-driven hostility, outspokenness, rage, protests, and emotions than the topic of Israel. The typical American university is a risky place to freely speak your mind about Israel.

For being such a small country, (approximately the size of New Jersey geographically, and with a population equal to New York City with 8 million-plus), Israel gets unprecedented news coverage across the world. The tiny nation is in the headlines every week—and has been for decades. Everyone seems to have a conviction about Israel, whether pro or con, informed or ignorant, politically charged or personally tailored. One recent example is when the United States decided to move its embassy from Tel Aviv to Jerusalem in May, 2018. Such a move formally recognized Jerusalem as the capital of Israel. Every corner of the earth responded to the move, and with dissonant, resounding passion. The act unconsciously drew a line, or more like an irreparable fissure, in the sand, and made manifest heretofore unforeseen loyalties.

Admittedly the topic of Israel today is a complex issue as it is being discussed and debated out in the world, on the news channels and talk shows, in the public school classroom, out on the streets and in the open air. Those discussions are typically fueled by politically motivated conventional narratives and not much factual data. So those conversations tend to generate more second-hand smoke than renewable energy. Lots of people are simply ignorant of foundational truths when it comes to Israel and the Jews. One of the main areas of widespread ignorance is regarding Israel's history, particularly its ancient history.

For the Christian who believes in the truthfulness and the authority of the Bible, the topic of Israel is straightforward and not confusing. That is the point of this book—to lay out the basic facts about Israel: its origin, history, status today and future existence, in addition to the proper Christian attitude toward Israel and the Jews—all from a biblical point of view. Not coincidentally this book is titled, *What the Bible Says about Israel.* After all, the entire Bible is about Israel and the Jews! Israel is mentioned over 2,500 times in the Bible! The Old Testament events happened in Israel between YHWH (God's name in Hebrew, the language of the Israelites) and the Jews. And the New Testament is all about a Jewish Messiah who was born, raised, ministered and died in Israel and who will one day rule the whole world...from the city of Jerusalem...in Israel! The Bible has a clear position on Israel and it is the final, authoritative word on the topic. We will now begin the first chapter with a survey of Israel's origin as delineated in Genesis, the first book of the Hebrew Bible.

To aid the reader, an Appendix with fifteen maps of Israel and the Promised Land are included in the back of the book. The maps are in chronological order and cover 6,000 years of world history, highlighting the status of the boundaries of the Promised Land, relative to Israel in each distinctive era.

1

The Origin of the Nations

It is not uncommon today to hear people say that the nation of Israel became a state in 1948. For people who don't know history (or the Bible), that statement can be incredibly misleading and misunderstood. Something significant and historical did transpire in 1948, but technically it was not the origin of a country called Israel. The proper way to say it is, "In 1948 the modern nation of Israel was re-established into a portion of their original land that God gave them after centuries of being subjugated, displaced and scattered throughout the globe." Israel did not begin to exist in 1948. Israel has existed as a nation in perpetuity and continuity for about 3,500 years.

It is true that as a nation they haven't always resided in the land God gave to them, as they lived as strangers in Egypt for 400 years and as exiles in Babylon for seventy years. Yet, as a homogenous, identifiable nation of people they have remained intact for nearly four millennia. That pretty much makes them the oldest nation on earth! Don't believe it? The proof? Here's an easy test; ask yourself a few simple questions: do you know any Hittites today? Name one. Are there any Girgashites or Hivites that live in your neighborhood? Or, what is the guy's name that started the nation of China? When was he born? Or the guy who started Japan or the Republic of San Marino? The fact is there is no nation on earth older than Israel. To a man—Abram—we know when the nation of Israel began. That cannot be said of any other nation that exists today. This is the story of the Bible, and here Genesis is our guide.

Before there were Nations

Today in 2020 we have about 193 nations.[1] That number fluctuates from decade to decade, century to century. Have you ever wondered, "How long have we had these nations? When did they all begin? What nation was first? Who made them? What defines a nation?" Amazingly, the Bible answers all these questions, and very specifically. As a matter of fact, only the Bible answers such questions—all the other religions, ideologies and philosophies of the world cannot answer these most basic questions. Take for example the most common ideology on planet earth today—evolution. When does evolution think all these nations arose? And why? The answer? By chance, without purpose and who knows when…and who cares? Chance has no purpose. Scripture, on the other hand, gives a clear purposeful theology of the history of earth and the origin of the nations.

Consider another example from a secular source representing a widespread view on this topic which dogmatically asserts that nations as we know them today did not exist prior to the 1500s, for before that time "most

---

[1] Although, there are around 6,000 national groups that exist who currently don't have recognized autonomy as independent states; James Minihan, *Encyclopedia of the Stateless Nations* (Westport, CT: Greenwood Press, 2002), xx.

people did not consider themselves part of a nation; they rarely left their village and knew little of the larger world…most people lived in small villages; they paid tithes to feudal landlords, didn't travel, and cared little for anything beyond the village."[2] Contrary to this popular, yet erroneous view, the Bible clearly explains history accurately when it describes precisely where nations came from.[3]

The first verse in the first chapter of the Bible tells us when world history began. "In the beginning God created the heavens and the earth" (Gen 1:1). The prophet Moses wrote the book of Genesis around 1400 BC. God gave him direct revelation of how everything began and God also gave Moses reliable tradition and history that was preserved by the faithful who wrote things down in formal records, or books, called the *toledoth* (cf. 2:4; 5:1; 6:9; 10:1; 11:10; 25:12). God revealed to Moses that He created the world in six real days, with humans—the apex of His creation—made in God's image on the sixth day. God declared this reality to the whole nation of Israel in Moses' day when He gave the Ten Commandments on the top of Mount Sinai. God said to Moses and all the people in attendance that day, "For in six days the LORD made the heavens and the earth, the sea and all that is in them, and rested on the seventh day; therefore the LORD blessed the sabbath day and made it holy" (Exod 20:11).

Moses believed God made the world in six days because that is what God told him that day (Exod 20:1). The Jews

---

[2] "The Rise of the Nation-State," sparkenotes.com, 2020, SparkNotes LLC.
[3] For a scholarly examination from an archaeological point of view validating the veracity of the Bible's explanation of Israel's origin, see James K. Hoffmeier's, *Ancient Israel in Sinai: The Evidence for the Authenticity of the Wilderness Tradition* (New York: Oxford University Press, 2005).

listening to Moses that day believed God made the world in six days. All the Old Testament prophets—from Samuel to Malachi—who read Moses believed the world was made in six days just as Moses wrote. Jesus, the Apostles, all the Jews of Jesus' day, and the entire early church believed God made the world in six days just as described in Genesis 1, thanks to the authoritative, impeccable history of Moses. They believed it because Genesis is reliable, inspired, true history.

According to God's inspired historical account, Genesis, the first two people God made were Adam and Eve (Gen 3:17, 20; cf. Mark 10:6). They brought forth Cain, Abel, Seth and many other children (5:4). Adam lived to be 930 years old (Gen 5:5), was blessed by God, and so produced many offspring in his lifetime. His children had many offspring and people began to populate the earth as God had planned. This went on for centuries until the days of Noah (6:1). Based on biblical chronology as revealed in Genesis chapters 5, 10, 11, I Kings 6:1 and many other biblical references, it's quite clear that Adam was created around 4,000 BC. From Genesis it can be determined that Noah lived around 2,500 BC, being the tenth in descent from Adam (5:28-29).

From the time of Adam in the beginning until the days of Noah there was only one nation on earth, or one people before God the Creator (Gen 4:26). That is a period of 1,500 years. There was one religion—the worship of Elohim (Gen 9:8-17). There was only one language spoken (Gen 11:1). It wasn't until the days of Noah, after the Flood, that God created various nations.[4] Moses is clear on this when he

---

[4] "During the 350 years that remained to Noah after the Flood, his family created a political universe as evidenced by the systematic appearance of Sumerian city-states and the voluminous Sumerian King-List. We still live in the outer precincts of that universe"; John D. Pilkey, *A Mesopotamian Timeline: Volume IVR* (Anacortes, WA: S. Marshall, 2018), 18.

wrote, "These are the families of the sons of Noah, according to their genealogies, by their nations; and out of these the nations were separated on the earth after the flood" (Gen 10:32). Distinct nations did not begin until God created them from the loins of Noah's three sons, Shem, Ham and Japheth (Gen 10:1; 11:1). For 1,500 years, from the days of Adam to Noah, there was just one nation called "the earth" (Gen 6:5).

The original regents of this universal domain called "earth" were Adam and Eve, for in the day God created them He gave them the mandate to "subdue," "rule" and "fill the earth" (Gen 1:27). They abdicated and forfeited their role as co-rulers through sin and rebellion. They became incapable of justly mediating God's power and rule over the earth. Despite their compromise, God would still see His initial mandate fulfilled of having a human mediator to rule over the whole earth on His behalf. That Mediator was the promised Messiah (Gen 3:15). Until that Messiah would come one day in glory to rule on the earth (Ps 89:19-29), God would manage His will upon the earth through fallen humanity via nations, various mediatorial agencies and the biblical covenants.

We All Came from Noah

Fifteen hundred years into world history, God, by His sovereign discretion, created nations upon the earth during the life of Noah. The first nine chapters of Genesis focus on the one world God created—the universal race of humanity. The radical shift from one monolithic human race (described in Genesis 1-9) to the diversity of nations (introduced in Genesis 10-11) was one main way God chose to mitigate against a united sinful humanity that chose to thwart His original command to "fill the earth," as they instead "settled" in one place (Gen 11:1-2). Beginning in Genesis 10, God zooms in on one particular man, family and nation—Abram, the Hebrew (Gen 14:13) and the Jews of Israel. These "Hebrew" people will occupy the main stage for the rest of Old Testament history, all the way up until the birth of the Jewish Messiah in Israel.

Genesis 10 introduces the three sons of Noah (Shem, Ham and Japheth) after the flood. They were real men—and the whole human race came from their loins...including you and me. This chapter is famously known as "The Table of Nations," and for good reason—it mentions the word "nations" at least six times. "The Table of Nations" is absolutely unique when it comes to ancient literature. There is nothing like it. Liberal theology frequently alleges that the Bible stories in Genesis are not original (or historical) but rather are hysterical and were borrowed from other, preexisting, ancient literary sources like *Enuma Elish*, the Babylonian creation myth from the Bronze Age, or the Akkadian myth, *Atra-Hasis*, and were adapted later by the Jewish community as fiction to give meaning to their ever-evolving Neanderthal religion of monotheism. As a matter of fact, the liberals tell us, pretty much the whole of the Old Testament is myth borrowed from somewhere else. But not so with the "Table of Nations." It has no parallel or equal anywhere in history; and it is history. And the critics of the Bible don't like that.

At first blush Genesis 10 looks like one of those scary, boring, irrelevant genealogies that you typically skip over when doing your daily Bible devotions as you read through your "whole" Bible in a year...because it's irrelevant or "does not give me the warm fuzzies." But that is not the case. It's not just a genealogy. It is loaded with significant information about world history, the origin of the nations, historical geography, the development of the races, political affiliations among tribes, and answers the supremely relevant question, "Where did Israel come from?" It actually answers the question, "Where did all the nations of the world come from?" for it lists no less than seventy different nations and families!

Genesis 10 skillfully unfolds in three distinct parts, listing fourteen descendants from Japheth (vv. 2-5), thirty from Ham (vv. 6-20), and twenty-six from Shem, the oldest of the three brothers (vv. 21-31). Of the seventy or so names Moses mentions in Genesis 10, not all the names are known today as to their exact derivation and allocation at the time God created these first nations. But there are several key truths we know for sure from this chapter.

First, we know that the Tower of Babel mentioned in Genesis 11 happened chronologically prior to Genesis 10, for the confusion of languages was one of the main catalysts God used to create the nations by scattering them abroad. So Genesis 10 should be read in tandem with Genesis 11:1-9 since together they provide a unified and complete historical context for one of the most revolutionary, disruptive and determinative periods of humanity's existence. Second, God used the confusion of languages to accomplish His original plan that humans would fill the whole earth (Gen 1:28; 11:8). Humanity's desire to gather in one place at the Tower of Babel and not spread throughout the earth as God commanded was an act of passive rebellion. Third, Genesis 10 is accurate in its ethnological delineation. Ethnology is a "science that deals with the division of human beings into races and their origin, distribution, relations, and characteristics."[5] Fourth, the list of names is not exhaustive, but the names given are important relative to their inevitable dealings with the nation of Israel who would eventuate as God's people from the loins of Shem and who, as the elect line, will occupy center stage of God's drama as unfolded throughout history, and the Old Testament, beginning in Genesis chapter 12 with Abram.

Moses' threefold breakdown of Genesis 10 based on Noah's sons is as follows:

(1) Japheth's descendants, mentioned first in verses 2-5, describe those who would be the progenitors "of the Gentile nations who located north and west of the land of Canaan. These would be the distant nations, the countries that represented the 'outer limits' of civilization for the average Old Testament Jew (Ps 72:8-10)."[6] These people continued to spread westward into Europe and eastward into India.[7]

(2) Moses then gives more attention to Ham's descendants in verses 6-20, including the perennial future enemies of Israel, namely the Egyptians, the Canaanites, the Assyrians and Babylon. Special attention is given to Nimrod as well, for he was the impetus behind the rebellion at Babel and the progenitor of false religion. The city of Babel eventually became Babylon, the

---

[5] Merriam-Webster.com, "Ethnology."
[6] Warren Wiersbe, *The Wiersbe Bible Commentary: The Complete OT in One Volume* (Colorado Springs, CO: David. C. Cook, 2007), 50.
[7] John Phillips, *Exploring Genesis* (Grand Rapids, MI: Kregel Publications, 1980), 96.

pagan nation that overcame God's people in
Judah (c. 605-539 BC), and who will again, at the
end of the age, rise to power and overwhelm
God's people during the Great Tribulation (Rev
16-18).

(3) Finally comes Shem's descendants (Gen 10:21-
31). Shem is the ancestor of the peoples known
as the Semites, a strain of Shemites who spoke
Semitic languages. The line of Shem is the line
of Abraham, Israel, and eventually the Messiah
(Luke 3:23-36; Gal 3:6-8). As such, Moses gives
it strategic attention with ethnological as well as
geographic significance. "Shem is usually
mentioned first, but he's listed last this time so
that the narrative can move right into the story
of Babel and the genealogy of Abraham, who
descended from Shem (11:10 ff.). Five sons are
mentioned, but the emphasis is on the family of
Arphaxad because he was the grandfather of
Eber (10:24). Abraham, the father of the
Hebrew nation (the father of the Jews; Matt 1:1;
Luke 3:8), came from the line of Eber, and his
story begins in chapter 12."[8] As to geographic
importance, "the portion of the earth occupied
by the descendants of Shem (10:21-31)
intersects the portions of Japheth and Ham and
stretches in an uninterrupted line from the
Mediterranean Sea to the Indian Ocean. It
includes Syria (Aram), Chaldea (Arphachshad),

---

[8] Wiersbe, *Commentary*, 51.

parts of Assyria (Asshur), of Persia (Elam), and of the Arabian Peninsula (Joktan)."[9]

A simple summary of how these first seventy nations dispersed from their three-fold point of origin (in relation to the land of Israel) is the "Japhethites migrated westward, the Hamites, south by southwest, and the Semites, south by southeast."[10]

Much more could be said about Genesis chapter 10, but the main point is that it, along with chapter 11, provides a unique, reliable, Spirit-inspired account of how the nations of the world first came into existence.[11] The nations of the world were created specifically and purposefully by God at a definitive time in recent world history, exactly as Genesis describes. Nations are not temporary pointless or purposeless secretions of deep evolutionary development, nor are they mere social constructs issuing from humanity's natural tribal instincts of self-preservations as some pagan sociologists suggest. The nations were created directly by God. Moses states this truth categorically in 1400 BC when he wrote: "the Most High gave the nations their inheritance, when He separated the sons of man" (Deut 32:8). The prophet Amos also reaffirmed this truth and the validity of Genesis 10's historical precision in 750 BC (Amos 9:7). The nations of the world came into being exactly according to God's plan and in accord with His sovereign established parameters, with Israel

---

[9] *The New Unger's Bible Dictionary*, ed. Merrill Unger (Chicago: Moody Press, 1988), 1176.

[10] *The Reformation Study Bible: Condensed Edition, ESV*, ed. R. C. Sproul (Orlando, FL: Reformation Trust Publishing, 2017), 22.

[11] Those interested in a fascinating, deeper study on the origins of the nations as described by Genesis 10-11 see John Pilkey's, *A Designed World: The Monogenesis of Man from Noah's Family*, published by Ross S. Marshall, 2017.

rising front and center among them all, being the vehicle by which God would bring the Messiah, and salvation, to the whole world (cf. John 4:42; Acts 17:26-27).

God Promises to Make Abram a Nation

Many Bible teachers say Genesis 12 is one of the most "pivotal" chapters in Genesis, if not the whole Old Testament. That is not to say it is the most "important," for every chapter in the Bible is equally important, for "all Scripture" is inspired by God (2 Tim 3:16). By "pivotal" we mean impactful or "loaded" in terms of its long-term, universal and even eternal implications, for in Genesis 12 God initiated one of His greatest acts of redeeming grace that would extend to all humanity for all the ages—and that is not an overstatement. For in this chapter God initiates the Abrahamic Covenant. One could say that the rest of the Bible is a commentary or detailed unfolding of the promises God laid out in the Abrahamic Covenant. The Abrahamic Covenant is so significant that it is repeated to Abram and his descendants at least twenty times in Genesis alone.[12]

Chapter 12 takes place around 2,100 BC. Abram is a seventy-five-year old pagan and idol-worshiper living in Haran, some 400 miles north of Shechem in Canaan. YHWH appeared to Abram making this monumental promise to him:

> [1] Now the LORD said to Abram,
> "Go forth from your country and from your relatives and from your father's house,
>> to the land which I will show you;

---

[12] 12:1-3, 7-9; 13:14-18; 15:1-18; 17:1-27; 22:15-19; 26:2-6, 24-25; 27:28-29, 38-40; 28:1-4, 10-22; 31:3, 11-13; 32:22-32; 35:9-15; 48:3-4, 10-20; 49:1-28; 50:23-25.

2 and I will make you a great nation, and I will bless you, and make your name great;
 and so you shall be a blessing;
3 and I will bless those who bless you, and the one who curses you I will curse.
 And in you all the families of the earth shall be blessed" (Gen 12:1-3).

Standing out as the Mount Everest of the Old Testament promises, this short passage has monumental implications. Let's look at several. First note that God spoke directly and audibly with Abram. God rarely does that. That is not the norm. In six thousand years of world history God spoke this way infrequently and usually only to select prophets. In the first 1,500 years of world history, from Adam to Noah, God did not routinely talk audibly to people. He did give direct revelation to Noah and Abraham on occasion because they were prophets (Gen 6:13; 12:4; 20:7; 2 Pet 2:5). Near the end of his life, Abraham reiterates for us again, saying, "The LORD God of heaven…spoke to me, and swore to me" (Gen 24:7). Amazingly after speaking directly to Abram when he was in Haran, God actually appears to Abram when he arrives in Shechem! "Then the LORD appeared to Abram" (12:7).

This is an astounding statement because God is a spirit (John 4:24), invisible (1 Tim 1:17), and does not have a physical body (Luke 24:39); He is infinite (Ps 139:7) and cannot be confined to one space (1 Kings 8:27). In addition, God is so holy that no human can look upon Him and live. God told Moses: "no man shall see Me and live" (Exod 33:20). Fifteen hundred years later John the Apostle said the same thing: "No one has even seen God" (1 John 4:12, ESV). Nevertheless, "the LORD appeared" to Abram in Genesis 12. The LORD appeared to Abram on other occasions as well (cf. 17:1; 18:1). YHWH appeared to Abram in unique ways throughout his life because God was a friend of Abram (James 2:23) and Abram had a unique role in history: he would become the father of all who believe (Rom 4:16) and literally become the father of the nation of Israel, God's special people. There is no contradiction in the Bible either, for when it says no one can see God, it is referring to God the Father, who is and remains spirit. Jesus, who is God, did appear at times in a body or in theophanies. Jesus appeared as YHWH in Genesis 18 to Abraham. Jesus referred to this event in the Gospel of John when He proclaimed, "Abraham rejoiced to see My day" (8:56).

The second great truth to note from Genesis 12:1-3 is that God chose to bless Abram before Abram was saved, while he was a pagan idol-worshipper (Josh 24:2). And God chose to save Abram based on sheer, undeserved grace and mercy. Abram was made righteous by God's sovereign choice. Abram's salvation was a gift that he did not earn or deserve. God's goodness to Abram was gratuitous and magnanimous.

Abram lived in defiance of his Creator by worshipping other gods for seventy-five-plus years while he lived in his homeland of Ur in southern Mesopotamia (near old Babylon). His name, Abram, meant "exalted father." Sometime between the ages of seventy-five and eighty-six (Gen 16:16), the God of grace invaded his life and saved him (15:6). When he was ninety-nine God changed his name to Abraham. His new name, which meant "father of a multitude" (17:5), reflected the spiritual renewal God wrought in his heart and it also spoke of the promises God made to him in the covenant. Abraham was saved by grace, through faith, apart from works. As such, he is the exemplar of all who come to saving faith by God's unmerited mercy and grace. Abraham is showcased in the New Testament as a model of faith (Heb 11:8-10). Paul argues that Christians are justified by faith in God's Word just as Abraham was (Rom 4; Gal 3:8). God even gives the faith that is necessary to be saved as a gift, and that faith comes from hearing divine, supernatural revelation (Rom 10:17). God loves and saves sinners on His own volition and initiative. This is true of Old Testament saints as well as New Testament saints. God's salvation plan is always the same through the ages. As Paul states, "God demonstrates His own love toward us, in that while we were yet sinners, Christ died for us" (Rom 5:8).

The third truth to be aware of in Genesis 12 is that this account is not the first time God called Abraham to move to Canaan. Interestingly, Genesis 11:31 says that Abraham's father, Terah, "took Abram, his son, and Lot, the son of Haran, his grandson, and Sarai his daughter-in-law, his son Abram's wife; and they went out together from Ur of the Chaldeans in order to enter the land of Canaan; and they went as far as Haran, and settled there." According to this verse, before God spoke to Abraham in Genesis 12 when he was in Haran, God appeared to Abraham when he lived in Ur in the land of Mesopotamia, some 600 miles east and south of Haran. Apparently, God originally spoke to Abraham when he was in Ur and told him to go to a foreign land (Canaan) (Gen 15:7), and his father, Terah, agreed to go with him. They travelled as far as Haran and then stopped short of where God wanted Abraham to go. After Terah died, God "brought" Abraham the rest of the way, to the town of Shechem (Neh 9:7). Stephen recounts the two-stage revelation and move of Abraham to Canaan:

> The God of glory appeared to our father Abraham when he was in Mesopotamia, before he lived in Haran, AND SAID

> TO HIM, "DEPART FROM YOUR COUNTRY AND
> YOUR RELATIVES, AND COME INTO THE LAND
> THAT I WILL SHOW YOU." Then he departed from the
> land of the Chaldean, and settled in Haran. And from there,
> after his father died, God removed him into this country in
> which you are now living (Acts 7:2-4).

God wanted Abraham separated from his father, and that happened in Haran. After leaving his father behind in Haran and arriving in Canaan, Abraham was in compliance with God's command and God blessed him as a result (Gen 12:4-8; Heb 11:8).

A fourth truth in Genesis 12:1-3 to note is that this revelation is the introduction of the Abrahamic Covenant. God would later formally enact the covenant with an oath and blood sacrifice in Genesis 15 and then give the human stipulations of the covenant (i.e., circumcision) in Genesis 17. God later reaffirms and renews the covenant throughout Abraham's life and with his descendants Isaac (Gen 26:1-5) and Jacob (28:10-17). We will unpack the major implications of this foundational covenant in the following chapters.

A fifth truth about this covenant that jumps out from the text of Genesis 12 is the oft repeated refrain spoken by God, "I will." As God introduces the covenant, He says five times, "I will." It means this is a unilateral covenant initiated and upheld by God alone. The promises are contingent upon the character of God. God calls it, "My covenant" (Gen 17:4) and "an everlasting covenant" (17:13). It cannot be annulled or undone by man's unfaithfulness. Ultimately, this covenant will be fulfilled exactly as God intended. God repeats His five "I will" commitments to the covenant in Genesis 17 when He ratifies it with a sign (vv. 6-8). God will never revoke this covenant He made with Abraham and his descendants, the

Israelites (Rom 11:1-27). God did the same thing when He gave Israel the New Covenant 1,500 years later, in that situation saying "I will" nine times! (Ezek 36:23-30).

The sixth significant truth in Genesis 12 has to do with the content of God's promise to Abraham which is four-fold. (1) God first promises to make Abraham "a great nation" (v. 2). (2) Next God promises to bless Abraham personally. (3) Then God promises to punish Abraham's enemies. (4) And finally, God promises to bless all the families of the earth through Abraham's progeny. After receiving this four-fold promise, Abraham immediately "departed from Haran" (v. 4) and headed to "the land of Canaan" (v. 5). He travelled until he reached Shechem, which was right in the heart of "the Promised Land," forty miles north of Jerusalem. It was there at Shechem that the LORD appeared once again to Abraham and said, "To your descendants I will give this land" (v. 12:7). That was despite the fact that "the Canaanites were in the land" before Abraham arrived there (v. 6).

One could argue, "Hey, the Canaanites were there long before Abraham was—the land belongs to them, not Abraham and the Jews! The indigenous people have the rights to it! Those Jews have always been occupiers and imperialists!" That would be the politically correct thing to say today in our culture. But the fact of the matter is that God owns the Promised Land and always did and always will. God reminded Moses of this timeless reality, declaring, "all the earth is Mine" (Exod 19:5). God is the "Possessor of heaven and earth" (Gen 14:19). More specifically, God says "the land is Mine" (Lev 25:23) referring to the Promised Land. The pagan, idol-worshipping Canaanites were evil trespassers and intruders on God's property (Ezra 9:1). That's why God would eventually command the Israelites in the future to displace the Canaanites who polluted and bloodied God's precious property (Exod 23:28). God even went a step further and told Moses that He Himself would "send an angel before you, and I will drive out the Canaanites" (33:2; cf. Deut 7:1). If you want to blame someone for driving out the Canaanites from the land of Palestine, then blame God—the Creator and Judge of the universe (Josh 24:11). But blaming God is foolish and dangerous (Job 40:2).

Summary

In this chapter we answered the questions, "Where did the nations of the earth come from?" and "Where did the nation of Israel originate?" God's Word in the book of Genesis gave clear answers. God created all nations after the Flood, around 2,500 BC. All nations find their origin in the three sons of Noah. Before Noah there was only one people on earth, with one language. God created nations to disperse the peoples throughout the earth as He commanded Adam and Eve to do in the beginning. God called Abram out from all people to become the nation of Israel, through whom the Messiah would come to be the Savior of the world. God made a solemn covenant with Abram and He promised to fulfill it. The rest of the Bible after Genesis shows how God kept His word. Now on to chapter two to roll out the implications of the Abrahamic Covenant which God gave to the first Israelite.

2

God Created Israel

Biblical Covenants

In the next few chapters we will examine the details of the "everlasting" covenant God made with Israel as contained in the Abrahamic Covenant. But first let's clarify the definition of covenant according to the Bible. A biblical covenant is an agreement or pact between two parties with specific stipulations as well as responsibilities, blessings and sometimes consequences. A covenant is like a promise, but it is more than a promise. It can have prophetic elements to it, but it is more than a prophecy. Covenants can be between two people (Gen 14:13; 21:27), two nations (Josh 9:6) or between God and humanity (Gen 9:12). They can be conditional or unconditional; temporary or permanent; unilateral or mutual; universal or particular; natural or spiritual.

Biblical covenants were often enacted through an official rite like a blood sacrifice, hence the technical expression, "to cut a covenant" (Gen 21:27), formalized with an oath and memorialized through a corresponding sign or symbol, like the rainbow with the Noahic Covenant (Gen 9:17), circumcision for the Abrahamic (Gen 17), the sabbath for the

Mosaic (Exod 31:16) and communion for the New Covenant (Luke 22:20). Covenants between God and man are mentioned all throughout the Bible, from Genesis (6:18) to Revelation (11:19). Covenants are means God uses to manage His relationship and plans for humanity and history. The nature, format, properties, protocol and conditions of the biblical covenants were created and established directly by God; they were not borrowed from surrounding pagan nations living among the Israelites, like the Hittites, as liberal theologians insist is the case.

There are only five undisputed covenants mentioned in the Bible that God established with humanity: the Noahic, Abrahamic, Mosaic, Davidic and the New Covenant. Late in church history certain theologians proposed, or concocted, non-biblical covenants they call the "theological covenants." These include the covenant of redemption, the covenant of works and the covenant of grace. "Covenant" theologians employ these non-Scriptural covenants, often with greater emphasis than the clearly delineated biblical covenants, as an artificial paradigm or lens by which to interpret the Bible, many times in a non-literal or allegorical manner. Typically, the non-literal approach is wielded to dissolve the clear historical distinction between Israel and the Church and this method of fanciful interpretation used in such cases is called "covenantal hermeneutics" or something similar.[13] But these man-made notions are contrived and confuse the meaning and implications of the perspicuous God-given biblical covenants. What God has ordained is sufficient, therefore the artificial non-biblical "theological" covenants will not be a

---

[13] Kenneth Gentry, "The Collapse of the Universe; or the Collapse of Dispensationalism?," *Dispensationalism in Transition* (Vol. V, No. 2; February, 1992), 1.

part of our purview in discussing the Abrahamic Covenant.

God Promised to Make Abram a Great Nation

Now on to the details of the Abrahamic Covenant. It was noted earlier that the first promise of the covenant that God made to Abram was, "I will make you a great nation" (Gen 12:2). This assertion by God is breathtaking and loaded with implications for us today and especially informs the topic, and debate, about Israel. This divine declaration is the theme of this book! In 2,100 BC God promised to make the nation called "Israel."

God never promised to make the nation of America, or China, or Russia or a nation of modern Palestinian Arabs. But He *did* promise to make a nation called Israel. And because God promised it, it was guaranteed to happen. God is in control of the future. In fact, God determines—or creates—the future. YHWH Himself said, "I *am* God, and there is no one like Me, declaring the end from the beginning and from ancient times things which have not been done, saying, 'My purpose will be established, and I will accomplish all My good pleasure'" (Isa 46:9-10). So, the nation of Israel came into being because God willed it. Israel is a nation by the decree of the Almighty.

Genesis 13 on through the rest of the Old Testament explains how God fulfilled that promise. Where did Israel come from? God made them! How did He make them? That is clearly described in Genesis 13 through Joshua 24. Which brings us to the questions: "What constitutes a nation? What does a *bona fide* nation entail as far as fundamental elements?" At a minimum, a true nation needs three things: (1) governance; (2) borders/land; and (3) citizens. Governance refers to ordained authority structures or laws. Borders refers to fixed boundaries that give a people autonomy and identity in relation to other surrounding people so they can maintain a distinguishable and monolithic national character. Citizens refers to a consensus of those who rightfully and mutually occupy a given territory and who have a united national purpose. A simple way to say it is, to make a nation you need (1) laws, (2) land and (3) laity; or, (1) polity, (2) a place, and (3) people, or (1) Torah, (2) territory and (3) tenants.[14]

God Provides People for the Nation

God provides these very three essentials for Abraham as He turned the sole great patriarch into a nation. First, as to people or laity, Genesis 13-50 shows how God gave Abraham the descendants beginning with Isaac, his son (Gen 17:19). Isaac married Rebecca and God blessed her with twins about which God said to her: "two nations are in your womb...the older shall serve the younger" (Gen 25:23). Two entire nations would come from these two boys, Esau and Jacob! The younger was Jacob, Abraham's elect grandson. God would save Jacob and then change his name to Israel (Gen 32:28; 35:10) and reiterate the Abrahamic Covenant to Jacob (Gen 28:13). Jacob went on to have twelve sons who became "the twelve tribes of Israel," who then would multiply into a

---

14 This biblical model of what defines an autonomous nation of the world as described in the Pentateuch and Joshua in 1400 BC was in keeping with what was established at the United Nations Security Council in 1948 when the American UN representative formally delineated to the world the basic qualifications of a nation: "first, there must be a people; second, there must be a territory; third, there must be a government" (*Israel, The Church and the Middle East: A Biblical Response to the Current Conflict*, ed. Darrell Bock and Mitch Glaser [Grand Rapids: Kregel, 2018], 205); a fourth stipulation was noted which had more to do with a nation's function, not its constitution, namely: "there must be a capacity to enter into relations with other states of the world." Israel met this qualification as well (1 Kings 5:12), so even by the current standards of today, Israel was a *bona fide* nation when God established it in the days of Moses.

tribe of seventy people (Gen 46:27). In His providence, God would bring the first small clan of seventy Israelites to Egypt safely (Gen 46:3) where they would spend 400 years (Gen 15:13) incubating and multiplying as a people until they reached a population of over 600,000 males, plus women and children (Exod 12:37)—a company of probably more than two million! History proves that God was true to His Word—He turned one man, Abram, into a nation comprised of a multitude of people, the nation of Israel (Exod 1:7).

God Provides Laws for the Nation
As to the second needed element to have a nation, law or governance. God raised up a leader for the budding nation, Moses—Israel's first political, military and religious leader. Exodus 1-3 tells the true story of his birth and rise to power as God commissions Moses to lead His people, the Israelites, to the Promised Land, where they will officially become God's nation on earth. Before the people entered the land to possess, God worked with Moses for eighty years, fine-tuning his leadership skills, and in the latter forty years of that span God gave the Law (or *Torah*) directly to Moses on behalf of the people. This Law is what we know as the Ten Commandments (Exod 34:28), which was Israel's national Constitution. In addition, God gave them another 603 laws to govern Israelite civil and religious life (Deut 5:1).

God Provides Territory for the Nation
The third element of a nation is land or territory with definitive borders, and that is the story of Exodus 12 through Joshua 24, under the leadership of Moses and then Joshua. God was very specific here. YHWH told Abram to go "to the land which I will show you" (Gen 12:1). God specifically told him it was the "land of Canaan" (Gen 11:31) the area known

today as Israel and Palestine. God gave this land specifically to Abraham's descendants. God said to him, "To your descendants I will give this land" (Gen 12:7). Abraham's descendants are the Jews. God promised to give the Promised Land to the Jews (Deut 27:3).

When Abraham was about 86 years old, God repeated the promise and got more specific by giving the borders or dimensions of the land. God said, "To your descendants I have given this land, from the river of Egypt as far as the great river, the river Euphrates" (Gen 15:18). Fast-forward 600 years to 1400 BC and God gives general boundaries of Israel's Promised Land to Moses as well: "I will fix your boundary from the Red Sea to the sea of the Philistines, and from the wilderness to the River *Euphrates*; for I will deliver the inhabitants of the land into your hand, and you will drive them out before you" (Exod 23:31). A little later God would give Moses even more specific boundaries of the Promised Land, delineating its southern, northern, western and eastern borders by name (Num 32:33-42; 34:1-15). Remember, the land always belonged to God and He had sovereign rights over it; He was the Divine Landlord. He gave that plot of land to Israel to own and possess. Regarding the original borders decreed by God, what stands out is how vast the stretch was.[15] God said the Jews would have the rights to all the land from the Euphrates River to the River in Egypt! Abraham lived for 100 years in Canaan, and he never owned any of it except for a small portion of land he bought to bury his wife (Gen 23). After all, God specifically promised to give

---

[15] In addition to the east-west borders given in Genesis 15:18, nine times the Old Testament mentions what would be the north-south borders as "Dan to Beersheba" (Judges 20:1; 1 Sam 3:20; 2 Sam 3:10; 17:11; 24:2, 15; 1 Kings 5:5; 1 Chron 21:2; 2 Chron 30:50).

the land, all of it, not to Abraham, but to his descendants.

Moving forward to the days of Joshua in the 1300's BC, God begins to fulfill the land promise. God leads the Israelites, through General Joshua, into the land of Canaan to possess it. Joshua was charged with removing ten enemy nations, in their entirety, in order to possess the land. He was not completely successful though, for most of the twelve tribes failed to conquer the entire area allotted to their charge (Judges 1:19-36). As a result, from the very beginning Israel never actually realized the ideal borders God laid down to Abraham in Genesis 15:18. The closest they would get in Old Testament history was during the reign of Solomon, around 1000 BC, but even then "Israel did not possess all that land. The [pagan] kings merely acknowledged Solomon's sovereignty and paid tribute to him."[16]

In the days of Christ, Israel did not possess the original territory God allocated to them, for they had been displaced by various pagan empires, including Assyria, Babylon, Medo-Persia, Greece and Rome, from 722 BC until the New Testament period. Then in AD 70 Rome attacked the Jews, destroyed the Temple and Jerusalem and thousands of Jews were dispersed abroad, yet many remained in the land, including Jerusalem. Finally, in AD 135, Hadrian the Roman Emperor attacked (i.e., utterly destroyed) and rebuilt Jerusalem, renaming it Aelia Capitolina. He banished all Jews, by royal decree, from the area,[17] although many Jews remained in the land outside Jerusalem, especially in Galilee. In fact, there has always been a Jewish presence in Israel since 135 AD. But their presence usually found them to be an

---

16 Wiersbe, *Commentary,* 69; cf. 1 Kings 4:21.
17 Merrill C. Tenney, *The Zondervan Pictorial Encyclopedia of the Bible, Vol. 3* (Grand Rapids: Zondervan, 1976), 354.

unwelcomed minority or under the yoke of foreign oppressors.[18] From AD 135 until the 20th century, the Jews, or Israelites, would be scattered all throughout the world just as God warned them back in the days of Moses when He said, "I will scatter you among the nations" (Lev 26:33). But God said the scattering would only be temporary, for He would remember the Abrahamic Covenant and eventually bring all the Jews back to the Promised Land (Lev 26:42-44) for them to possess it once and for all, in the future under the reign of the Messiah, Jesus Christ (Ps 2; Ezek 47-48; Zech 12-14; 2 Thess 1:7-10). That day is yet to come!

Summary

This chapter showed how God faithfully fulfilled His first promise to Abraham in the covenant, namely, that He would make Abram a great nation. He did so by providing Abram with the required laity, land and laws. God provided people for the nation by multiplying descendants through the loins of Isaac and Jacob. During the 400 years in Egypt (1850-1450 BC), Israel grew from 70 to 2,000,000 people. God provided the nation's Constitution and Law through their first national leader, Moses. And God gave them land as they were led by Joshua to take the land God promised them. In the next chapter we will survey the second promise in the Abrahamic Covenant.

---

18 "The history of Jerusalem by no means terminated with Titus. Rebuilt in AD 135 as the Roman colony Aelia Capitolina, the city has since experienced nine major periods: Roman (continued), to 330; Byzantine, to 638; Arab, to 1099; Crusader, to 1187 (plus 1229-1244); Arab again, to 1516; Turkish, to 1917; British, to 1948; Jordanian, to 1967; and Israeli, to the present"; Tenney, *Pictorial Encyclopedia*, 486.

3

Abraham: The First Jew

Abraham was the first Jew. The Jews go by many different names in the Bible. Originally they were called Hebrews, then the sons of Jacob, then Israel and after the divided kingdom they were called Jews, which comes from the name Judah. On occasion they are called sons of Abraham. Abraham is the progenitor of the Jews and therefore the first Jew. As the first great Patriarch, Abraham was blessed by God.

God Blessed Abraham Spiritually
After promising to make Abram "a great nation," God next promises to bless him: "I will bless you, and make your name great" (Gen 12:2). In this chapter we will look at several ways God blessed Abraham in light of this promise. Abraham was indeed blessed by God during his lifetime in many ways, and even beyond the grave. We already saw how God would bless him by making him a "great nation." It takes a unique person, specially chosen by God, to be the progenitor of a nation, for God is the one who creates nations (Dan 2:20-21). Nations don't arise spontaneously, organically or by the sheer will of man. YHWH is completely sovereign over all the nations of all history; He "rules over the nations" (Ps 22:28). So, God blessed Abraham by making him a great nation—Israel, the

greatest nation that ever existed. Israel is the greatest nation that ever existed, not because of the humans who composed it, but rather because God was the true King of Israel, the divine despot: "Let Israel be glad in his Maker; let the sons of Zion rejoice in their King" (Ps 149:2).

Abraham was also blessed with the greatest gift a person can receive—spiritual salvation. At some point in his life after age seventy-five, Abraham became a believer, or justified (Rom 4:3). Everything about salvation is a blessing from God (Jonah 2:9)—from being elect in eternity past, to being called and wooed by God, His Word and His Spirit during this life prior to salvation, the moment of supernatural justification where the guilty sinner is pronounced "not guilty!" by God the Judge, to the guarantee of complete salvation through glorification and resurrection in the age to come (Rom 8:29-30). All these realities became true of Abram, the former idol-worshipper.

The many special appearances God made to Abraham throughout his life were unique blessings that most humans in history never experience (Gen 12:7; 15:17; 17:1; 18:1). Through those experiences, Abraham acquired special revelation from heaven which was a prerequisite to being saved. Sinful humans—and that's all of us—need divine revelation from God in order to acquire the needed faith that leads to salvation (2 Tim 3:15). Saving faith comes to us in only one way—as a gift from God (Eph 2:8) as a result of hearing the Word of God; that is through God-given divine, special, heavenly revelation, in whatever form it may come (Rom 10:17). And God blessed Abram with the gift of faith (Heb 11:8). No one can be saved apart from the faith that results from special revelation that is initiated and given by God as a gift. No one is saved through general revelation, natural theology, intuition, good works, good intentions, intelligence, family status, social status, man-made religion or any other human mechanism. True salvation is a blessing from God.

Another way God blessed Abraham spiritually in addition to saving him out of paganism is the ongoing grace God imparted to him throughout his long life. Even after being saved Abraham was a sinner…like all of us (1 Kings 8:46). He doubted God at times despite the covenant (Gen 15:2; 17:17). He once took matters into his own hands by asking his wife to lie to Pharaoh for him (Gen 12:13). He himself lied to King Abimelech of Gerar (Gen 20:2). He committed sexual immorality against his wife Sarah (Gen 16:4). Despite his failings, he remained God's friend and was considered by God to be an example of righteousness and faith (cf. Gal 3:6-7). Fittingly, Abraham is allocated more verses in the "Hall of Faith," with an uncontested ten, with Moses taking second place with seven (Heb 11:8-19). Ongoing grace and forgiveness for the believing sinner is indeed a great blessing. Believers of all ages are blessed by the ongoing reality that "where sin increased, grace abounded all the more"! (Rom 5:20).

God Blessed Abraham Physically

In addition to blessing Abraham spiritually, God also blessed him physically. Genesis 24:1 says plainly, "Now Abraham was old, advanced in age; and the LORD had blessed Abraham in every way." God blessed Abraham by granting him a rich, full, and even extraordinary life. God blessed Abraham with a long life. He lived to be 175! (Gen 25:7). "Abraham…died in a ripe old age, an old man and satisfied with life" (25:8). He outlived his wife, Sarah, who died at 127 (23:1). He lived longer than his son Ishmael who died at 137 (Gen 25:17). Compare Abraham's longevity to other Old Testament saints: Jacob (Israel) his grandson died at 147 (47:28); Joseph died at 110 (50:22); Levi died when he was 137 (Exod 6:16); Aaron was 123 (Num 33:39). Moses died at 120 (Deut 34:7), Joshua at 110 (24:29), and King David at 70 (2 Sam 5:4; 1 Kings 2:11).

God also blessed Abraham with wealth. Wealth is often portrayed in the Bible as a direct blessing from God (cf. Job 42:10, 12). After all, God is the One who enables any person to make money (Deut 8:18)—He's the dispenser of all good gifts, including income and material possessions (James 1:17). Even though Abraham was a sojourner and foreigner in the land of Canaan for 100 years, never acquiring any of the land there personally, except one small burial plot, God made him immensely wealthy. "Abram was very rich in livestock, in silver, and in gold" (Gen 13:2). He had servants, attendants, and flocks of all sorts.

Eliezer, Abraham's most trusted servant, testified of God's blessing upon his master Abraham, saying, "The Lord has greatly blessed my master, so that he has become rich; and He has given him flocks and herds, and silver and gold, and servants and maids, and camels and donkeys" (24:35; cf. 12:16). Abraham even had his own private army—318 fierce, highly trained fighting men, all born in his house (14:14). God's blessing upon Abraham was evident to all, and as such the many powerful indigenous chieftains of the day respected Abraham as a fellow sheik of influence, including Pharaoh, king of Egypt (12:16), Mamre the Amorite chieftain (14:13), Bera the king of Sodom (14:17), Melchizedek, king of Salem (14:18), and Abimelech king of Gerar (20:14). God had indeed "made his name great" as He had promised (12:2).

God's material blessing on Abraham was generational; his son Isaac was made wealthy: "the LORD blessed him, and the man became rich, and continued to grow richer until he became very wealthy; for he had possessions of flocks and herds and a great household, so that the Philistines envied him" (Gen 26:12-14). Jacob (Israel), Abraham's grandson, was also made rich by God (30:27-30; 43) and Jacob recognized this later in life, as he confessed, "the God of my father has been with me" (31:5). By God's grace, Jacob had accumulated a multitude of male and female servants, oxen, donkeys, goats, rams, cows, bulls, flocks, camels and more (31:17-18; 32:5, 14-15).

Finally, God blessed Abraham's personal and family life. Earlier it was noted that Abraham died an old man who was "satisfied." He was satisfied because he knew God, but part of his satisfaction came from his wife Sarah. Much of a married man's satisfaction is related to the quality of his wife. God wants a husband to enjoy his wife (Prov 5:18). "An excellent wife is the crown of her husband, but she who shames him is like rottenness in his bones" (Prov 12:4). And, "He who finds a good wife finds a good thing and obtains favor from the LORD" (Prov 18:22). Sarah was a good wife. Abraham and Sarah were married for seventy years or more! They had their spats like all married couples, but they were committed to each other, and Sarah proved to be a godly wife. She was an exemplary woman of faith who trusted in the promises of God (Heb 11:11). The New Testament holds her up as the model of a godly, quiet and submissive wife— one who pleases God (1 Pet 3:1-6). Sarah was a ready and willing helper to her husband, and hospitable to strangers (Gen 18:6). Abraham loved her and mourned and wept deeply when she died (23:2). She was a beloved mother as well to her son Isaac. Isaac had a hole in his heart when his mother died when he was just thirty-seven (Gen 24:67).

Another related blessing in Abraham's family life is the miracle of God opening Sarah's barren womb, enabling her to become pregnant at age ninety, long after the normal child-bearing years. Paul noted that at ninety, Sarah's womb was "dead" (Rom 4:19). Paul also noted that it would take a miracle of God for Sarah and Abraham to have a child (4:21). And that's exactly what God did. When Abraham was ninety-nine God told him his old wife was going to have a baby. Abraham "fell on his face and laughed" in disbelief (Gen 17:17). Shortly after that incident, Sarah overheard God talking to Abraham again saying she would have a baby and then she laughed hysterically at the absurd idea (18:12) and then lied about laughing (18:15). One year later Sarah gave birth to a son and named him Isaac, which means "laughter." So, twenty-five years after God first told Abram that He would make him a nation, God followed through with the promise by granting an heir to Abraham. The greatest blessing about Isaac's birth was that through his line the Messiah, Jesus, would eventually come as Savior of the world (Luke 3:23-34).

Summary
God fulfilled His promise in the Abrahamic Covenant when He told Abram, "I will bless you" (Gen 12:2). God blessed Abraham by making him a special nation. God blessed him by justifying him after he lived a pagan life for seventy-five years. God blessed Abraham by appearing to him many times and giving him special revelation. God blessed Abraham for 100 years by showing him ongoing grace with the forgiveness of sin as he stumbled morally and in many other ways. God

also blessed him with a long satisfying life, wealth and possessions, a believing wife, and an heir in his old age. In the next chapter we examine another promise in the covenant— blessing and cursing extended to others through Abraham.

4

God Protects Israel

So far, as we have examined the content of the Abrahamic Covenant, we have showed how God would make Abraham a great nation and secondly, how God would bless him personally. Now a third promise of the Covenant will be highlighted, which God speaks in Genesis 12:3:

> And I will bless those who bless you,
> and the one who curses [*qallelka*] you I will curse [*abaraka*],
> and in you all the families of the earth will be blessed.

Notice first in the promise that the word "curse" in English is actually two different Hebrew words. Ross summarizes the significance here:

> The two words for "curse"...are synonyms and thus overlap in their meanings. But *'arar*, the stronger of the two, means to impose a barrier or a ban, a paralysis on movement or other capabilities, or to remove from the place and power of blessing. *Qalal*, "treat lightly," means to hold in contempt, speak lightly, or curse. Anyone who disrespects and treats Abram and his faith lightly will thus be removed from the place of blessing. The wording records this threat as a necessary part of the outworking of the promises.

Consequently, Abram would be the channel of blessing for the whole world.[19]

Some different English translations capture the important distinction in the two words through more literal translations than what the NASB or KJV render:

> "and him who dishonors you I will curse" (ESV);
> "but the one who treats you lightly I must curse" (NET);
> "I will curse anyone who treats you with contempt" (CSB).

God Cursed Abraham's Enemies

As soon as God made this promise to Abraham, He fulfilled it graphically as seen in the latter part of Genesis chapter 12, for around this time there was a severe famine in the land of Canaan. Abraham decided to go to Egypt with his family to find relief. Abraham knew that the Egyptians were a dangerous people and that they might take his life upon arriving. Sure enough, as soon as they arrived in Egypt, Pharaoh's servants snatched Abraham's wife away because of her physical beauty.

Pharaoh tried to buy Sarah from Abraham. That infuriated God, who just made a covenant with Abraham, and so "the LORD struck Pharaoh and his house with great plagues" for taking Sarah (Gen 12:17). Pharaoh "dishonored" or "treated lightly" Abraham, so in return as God just promised, He literally "cursed" Pharaoh and his house with a plague. Pharaoh got the message and returned Sarah immediately and he had Abraham safely escorted away from his presence with all of his belongings.

Another example of God immediately honoring this promise of blessing those who bless Abraham is in Genesis

---

[19] Allen P. Ross, *Creation and Blessing: A Guide to the Study and Exposition of Genesis* (Grand Rapids: Baker Academic, 1998), 264.

14 when Abraham is drawn into an international skirmish when his nephew Lot was kidnapped. Moses sets the stage of the battle: four aggressor Mesopotamian kings, east of Canaan, near ancient Babylonia (modern day Iran), invaded and attacked five kings who lived south of the Dead Sea (i.e., the valley of Siddim)—five kings who were living in the land that God had already promised to give to Abraham's descendants, the Israelites. The four-fold eastern coalition were kings from Shinar, Ellasar, Goiim and Elam. King Chedorlaomer of Elam was the ring-leader of these evil imperialist invaders.

The five cities in the plain of Jordan, south of the Dead Sea, were Sodom, Gomorrah, Admah, Zeboiim and Zoar. Lot, Abraham's nephew, had been living in Sodom. For twelve years the five cities near the Dead Sea had been paying tribute (produce and money) to Chedorlaomer who had previously conquered their territory. In the thirteenth year the five cities rebelled—they were tired of being extorted by an evil oppressor who lived hundreds of miles away. One year after the rebellion, Chedorlaomer brought his three allies with him to punish the five kings who were not paying their dues and they invaded the valley of Siddim, by the Dead Sea, in the land of Canaan.

The four evil kings conquered and plundered Sodom and Gomorrah and kidnapped Lot. A fugitive was able to escape and inform Abraham that Lot had been taken captive. Abraham immediately mustered his standing army of 318 soldiers and led them on a long trek, over 120 miles going north in a surprise attack at night against Chedorlaomer and his allies, overtaking them and defeating them near Damascus. Abraham successfully recovered all that was stolen, including his nephew Lot. Abraham became a military hero.

How did Abraham, an aged man in his eighties, and his small band of 318 soldiers overtake and utterly defeat four time-tested kings and their experienced soldiers? God was on Abraham's side. He had just promised Abraham, "him who dishonors you, I will curse." Evil Chedorlaomer dishonored Abraham by taking Lot, one of his family members captive, and as promised, God cursed the four kings by giving them into Abraham's hand.

A few years later, when Abraham was ninety-nine, he journeyed with his wife Sarah to a desert region south of Judea in a town called Gerar, midway between the Dead Sea and the Mediterranean Sea. The king of Gerar was Abimelech. As Abraham entered Gerar, he lied to the people there saying Sarah was his sister—just as he lied to Pharaoh in Egypt. And so Abimelech the king took Sarah for himself by force. The God of Abraham immediately appeared to Abimelech in a dream and said, "Behold, you are a dead man because of the woman you have taken, for she is married" (Gen 20:3). Out of fear the king let Sarah go and pleaded for mercy. God spared the king's life. Here God was cursing a king who cursed Abraham. In this case, God was protecting Abraham and Sarah despite the fact that they lied to Abimelech. God's promise to bless those who blessed Abraham and curse his enemies was not contingent upon Abraham's perfection, or even his consistent obedience. God would fulfill His promises of the Abrahamic Covenant in spite of Abraham's faults. Amazing grace.

God Blessed Isaac and Jacob

These three preceding scenarios highlight God's faithfulness to His Word. He made a promise, and He kept it...literally and immediately. But God's promise to bless and curse was intended to extend beyond Abraham to his descendants—to his son Isaac, his grandson Jacob and his offspring. God's promise in effect was a promise to the nation of Israel itself. And that is the clear testimony of all Old Testament history. Israel, Abraham's offspring, became God's special people (Deut 7:7-9). God "married" the nation of Israel (Isa 54:5-8; Jer 2:2; 31:32; Hos 2:16). They were the apple of His eye (Deut 32:10); His elect nation (Isa 45:4); His holy people (Exod 19:6); His flock (Ezek 34); His own possession (Deut 7:6); His beloved and adopted children (Ezek 16). He was committed to protecting and blessing them.

God gave Abraham and Sarah a promised son, Isaac, who would perpetuate the promises of the Abrahamic Covenant. When Isaac became a father, he blessed his son Jacob, passing on God's promises of the covenant. With God's sanction he said to Jacob,

> May peoples serve you,
> And nations bow down to you;
> Be master of your brothers,
> And may your mother's sons bow down to you.
> Cursed be those who curse you,
> And blessed be those who bless you (Gen 27:29).

Clearly God's promise to bless friends and curse enemies extended to Abraham's offspring, and in particular the nation of Israel. Jacob literally becomes Israel when God changes his name.

"Jacob" is a Hebrew word that means "the one who grasps," a usurper and supplanter, and by extension, "deceiver" (Gen 25:26; 27:36). That is how Jacob lived his life for the first forty years; deceiving those around him, including family. Then he had a special encounter with God where he was humbled and was willing to submit to God. At that point God gave him a new name, Israel, meaning, "one who strives with God" (Gen 32:28), thus reorienting Jacob's life from that point on as one who would strive alongside God, not against God. Jacob would not resist God as he had done previously, but welcomed the will of God in his life, which amounted to him being the direct progenitor of the twelve tribes of Israel (Exod 24:4), i.e., the nation of Israel.

God Cursed the Enemies of Israel

Fast-forward 500 years from the life of Jacob to the days of Moses in 1,440 BC. The Hebrews (Israelites) had been enslaved, deprived and even brutalized by the pagan nation of Egypt and their ruthless taskmasters, the Pharaohs, for nearly 400 years. The Israelites, who were in bondage, cried out to God. Their cry "rose up to God. So, God heard their groaning; and remembered His covenant with Abraham, Isaac and Jacob...and took notice of them" (Exod 2:23-24). God made a promise to bless Israel and curse her enemies; so, He did. God cursed Egypt with ten plagues and destroyed Pharaoh and his elite chariot army, drowning them in the sea. This was a specific fulfillment of the promise God made to Abraham in 2100 BC when God told him about the oppressive Egyptians, "I will judge the nation [who enslaves Israel] whom they will serve, and afterward they [the Hebrew slaves] will come out with many possessions" (Gen 15:14). As a result, Moses led near two million Hebrew slaves out of Egypt into the wilderness of Sinai, *en route* to the Promised Land.

After wandering for forty years in the wilderness, travelling from Sinai toward the Promised Land, Moses led the Israelites to the plains of Moab on the east of the Jordan River. Here the Spirit of God spoke through Balaam as he invoked a blessing upon the nation of Israel, saying in part,

> How fair are your tents, O Jacob, Your dwellings, O Israel…
> God…will devour the nations who are his adversaries,
> And will crush their bones in pieces,
> And shatter them with his arrows….
> Blessed is everyone who blesses you,
> And cursed is everyone who curses you (Num 24:5-9).

Here God repeats the promise He made to Abraham in Genesis 12 and applies it directly to the nation of Israel. What is amazing with this iteration of the promise is that Israel as a nation had been largely disobedient for forty years towards God in the wilderness. After seeing first-hand YHWH's deliverance of the nation through a series of miracles at the time of the Exodus (Exod 7-12), the Israelites responded with ceaseless grumbling (Exod 16), rebellion (Num 16), idolatry (Exod 32), and unbelief (Exod 14:10-12).

Despite Israel's failings and repeated disobedience, God blessed Israel all throughout their forty years of wandering in the wilderness. Just before his death as he stood across from the Promised Land, Moses reminded the Israelites of God's mercy, grace and faithfulness toward them as a nation: "For the LORD your God has blessed you in all that you have done; He has known your wanderings through this great wilderness. These forty years the LORD your God has been with you; you have not lacked a thing" (Deut 2:7). Instead of abandoning the fickle, capricious, discontent people, God responds by reassuring them of His promise to bless those who bless Israel and to curse their enemies. This is amazing grace.

The amazing grace of God's protection and blessing

toward a compromised Israel continues all throughout Old Testament history, from 1400 BC to the fifth century BC, just prior to the inter-testamental period of revelatory silence.[20] God blessed Israel as they entered the Promised Land under the leadership of Joshua. God cursed the Canaanites who cursed Israel, evidenced by God allowing Israel to win military battle after military battle over the course of fifteen years, enabling them to possess the land God had promised them, as far south as Beersheva to Dan in the north.

With God's help, Israel displaced the seven groups of enemies that occupied the land (Josh 24:11). "The LORD gave Israel all the land which He had sworn to give their fathers, and they possessed it and lived in it. And the LORD gave them rest on every side, according to all that He had sworn to their fathers, and no one of all their enemies stood before them; the LORD gave all their enemies into their hand. Not one of the good promises which the LORD had made to the house of Israel failed; all came to pass" (Josh 21:43-45). God blessed Israel in the days of Joshua and cursed Joshua's enemies.

God blessed Israel during the distressing days of the Judges. From 1390 BC to 1050 BC God raised up twelve judges, or deliverers, on behalf of the Israelites whenever they were in national distress (Judges 2:16). God delivered them despite their pathological, cyclical, proclivity toward disobedience, as "they forsook the LORD God of their fathers, who had brought them out of the land of Egypt" (2:12).

---

[20] Two excellent surveys of Israel's history from a biblical and scholarly perspective are, *A Survey of Israel's History*, by Leon J. Wood (Grand Rapids, MI: Zondervan Academic, 1986) and Walt Kaiser's, *A History of Israel: From the Bronze Age through the Jewish Wars* (Nashville, TN: B & H Publishers, 1998).

God also blessed Israel during the time of the united monarchy from Saul to Solomon (1050 BC to 930 BC). Israel's first three kings (Saul, David and Solomon) had some serious personal, spiritual and moral defects; nevertheless, because God said He would bless Israel and curse Israel's enemies, that is exactly what happened. God remained true to His promises, even when His people were unfaithful. Just like with us as believers today when "we are faithless, He remains faithful" (2 Tim 2:13). We are no better than sinful saints who came before us. Israel reached its greatest level of prosperity and expansion under the rule of Saul, David and Solomon. God blessed Israel and cursed her enemies of the day, most notably the Philistines. At his peak, King David enjoyed the blessing of God for "the LORD had given him rest from all his enemies all around" (2 Sam 7:1).

God preserved Israel during the time of the divided monarchy, the darkest days of Israel's history (930 BC to 600 BC). Even though powerful, evil pagan kings like Sennacherib of Assyria and Nebuchadnezzar of Babylon tried to utterly destroy Israel, God preserved a remnant in the land of Promise. God preserved Israel as a nation despite wholesale, ongoing rebellion toward their God YHWH. Then from about 600 BC to 530 BC God protected Israel during the days of the Babylonian captivity. God would eventually curse Babylon for attacking the Jews (Dan 5), showing favor to exiled Jews and then allowing them to return to their homeland of Jerusalem to reconstruct the city (Ezra), the Temple (Hag 2:3) and the wall (Neh 1) (530 BC to 400 BC). God continued to protect and bless the nation of Israel from the time of Malachi to the New Testament (400 BC to 4 BC). As many prominent ancient nations of history, such as the Philistines, Hittites, and Amalekites, vanished into nonexistence (Deut 25:17-19), Israel continued on in continuity and perpetuity under the protective hand of the God of Abraham.

What about Now?

The Old Testament makes it clear that God would be true to His promise to bless Israel and curse Israel's enemies up until the time of the last Old Testament prophet. But what about during the time of Christ and the beginning of the Church? Would God continue to bless Israel, the very people who rejected Jesus, God's promised Messiah? Was there an expiration date to the promise given in Genesis 12:3. After all, the Bible clearly says about Jesus the Savior: "He came to His own, and those who were His own did not receive Him" (John 1:11). This verse says that "His own", the Jews, rejected Him. Many influential evangelical Bible teachers extrapolate this verse and extend it as a general truism that applied to the early church and throughout all Church history, thus concluding that God has rejected the Jews as a nation. He has turned from the nation Israel in favor of the spiritual nation of the Church. Genesis 12:3 indeed had an expiration date for the nation of Israel. All Old Testament promises, they allege, made to Israel are now transferred to, realized, and subsumed in Christ's cosmopolitan Church. Therefore, today Israel has no special standing or place in God's program, nor will they in the future. Israel then is just another unbelieving nation among many.

Sadly, the notion that Israel has no special place in God's present or future program is widespread in the church.[21] That

---

21 Thank God for the flurry of recent books by a cohort of excellent Evangelical scholars attempting to counter this longstanding and detrimental hegemonic trend, books such as *Israel, the Church and the Middle East*, ed. by Darrell L. Bock and Mitch Glaser, 2018; *Eternal Israel* by

is a reality due in part to influential Christian teachers of the past who wielded an allegorical hermeneutic when speaking of Israel's unfulfilled promises, changing the literal promises which were originally given by God to Israel and then, through creative exegetical gymnastics, massaging them, symbolically or allegorically, to now apply to the New Testament church. Augustine began doing this in the fifth century. Luther, the influential German Reformer, did the same with the Jews and the nation of Israel. He clearly taught that God had abandoned Israel:

> It seemed to him that God had deserted the Jews, leaving them to wander homeless without a land or temple of their own. And if this was God's attitude, then one might with good conscience ignore the Jews. Why would God desert his own people if he did not despair of them? He had rejected them and turned his attention to the "new Israel," the Christian church. Luther thus accepted the existing notion that the promise given to Jews was now transferred to Christians.[22]

Despite Augustine and Martin Luther's highly influential allegorical displacement of Israel as God's special people, the Bible teaches otherwise. Genesis 12 still stands true, and literally so. God has not abandoned the nation of Israel. He will continue to "bless them" and "curse" their enemies. Consider a few reasons why. First, God's commitment to Israel was originally made to them based on an oath God made with Himself, not based on the goodness, worthiness or behavior of Israel; the promise was unilateral and uncon-

---

Barry E. Horner, 2018; *What Should We Think About Israel,* ed. by J. Randall Price; and *Forsaking Israel,* ed. by Larry Pettegrew, 2020.
[22] Eric W. Gritsch, "Was Luther anti-Semitic?" ChristianHistoryInstitute.org, 1993.

ditional (Gen 15; Deut 7:8; Luke 1:73; Heb 6:13).[23] Second, God's promise to Israel was "everlasting " (Gen 17:7) and "forever" (Gen 13:15; Exod 32:13). It had no expiration date. God said He would be true to Israel as long as there would be a sun, moon and stars shining in the sky (Jer 31:35-36). Third, Israel is God's "elect" nation (Isa 45:4)—God's election is irreversible and irrevocable and not contingent upon human behavior. Speaking of being elect of God, Paul says about Israel's status: "the gifts and the calling of God are irrevocable" (Rom 11:29). Fourth, God said many times that Israel would not disqualify themselves even if they compromise or disobey; God said their consequences in such cases would be temporary and partial chastening, not utter rejection or total abandonment (Lev 26; Deut 28-30; Rom 11:19-26). Fifth, God explicitly said that Israel will soften in the future, in the last days, and turn to the Messiah as a nation (Isa 19:16-25; Zeh 12:10; Rom 11:26; Rev 7:1-8; 12:13-17). Sixth, the New Testament never calls the Church the "new Israel" or "Spiritual Israel." In the New Testament, the word "Israel" and the word "Jew" always retain their normal meaning which is inextricably linked to ethnic Judaism.[24]

In light of the above, it is clear that Israel is still special to God and has a place in His program. As a matter of fact, Paul warns arrogant Christians not to despise or look down upon

---

23 MacArthur correctly notes, "The choosing of Israel as a holy nation set apart for God was grounded in God's love and His faithfulness to the promises He had made to the patriarchs, not in any merit or intrinsic goodness in Israel"; *The MacArthur Study Bible* (Nashville: Thomas Nelson, 1997), 261. After all, God chose Abram, the first Jew, and gave him the promise, before he was justified.

24 "No clear-cut example of the church being called 'Israel' exists in the NT or in ancient church writings until A.D. 160. Galatians 6:16, where 'the Israel of God' can and probably does refer to some group other than the church as a whole, is no exception"; Robert L. Thomas, *Revelation 1-7: An Exegetical Commentary* (Chicago: Moody Press, 1992), 476.

unbelieving Jews, otherwise God may be provoked and "cut off" those who mock and degrade His unique people, the nation of Israel (Rom 11:22). So even today, in ways we may not even be aware of, God will continue to bless those who bless Israel and He will curse those who curse them.

Summary

From the above survey of Old Testament history beginning in 2100 BC with Abraham down to the close of the Old Testament in 400 BC, and even up to the present day, it is apparent that God kept His promises stipulated in the Abrahamic Covenant to the nation of Israel, as God, time and time again, blessed those who blessed Israel and cursed those who cursed them. God's faithfulness to Israel was not contingent upon Israel's worthiness, impressive spirituality, or even their ability to keep the covenant. In fact, they didn't keep the covenant (Hos 8:1). God's faithfulness to Israel was based on His unconditional election of Israel and also because of His holy name which He could not violate (Deut 7:7-9; Ezek 36:22-23). For when He ratified the covenant with Abraham, He did so based on an inviolable oath He made with Himself! (Heb 6:13-17). In Ezekiel God accentuates His unique love that He set on Israel as His elect nation when He said that Israel was the "center" of the world (5:5).

Having seen several examples of God staying true to the third promise in the Abrahamic Covenant, we now turn to the next chapter to examine a fourth related promise—God's commitment to bless the ends of the earth through the lineage of Abraham and the nation of Israel.

5

Israel Will Bless the World

The fourth blessing of the Abrahamic Covenant is intrinsically related to the promise just examined in the last chapter. One flows from the other. Genesis 12:3 reads,

> And I will bless those who bless you,
> and the one who curses [*qallelka*] you I will curse [*abaraka*],
> and in you all the families of the earth will be blessed.

God promised Abraham that "in you all the families of the earth will be blessed." This is a staggering promise when considering all its implications. Through one fallen, old man—so old he was "as good as dead" (Heb 11:12)—God would bless the whole world for generations to come, until the culmination of world history. And the nature of that blessing was of the highest order. This was a potent promise.

The promise was also cryptic when it was first revealed. Many of the details of how the promise would unfold and be fulfilled came incrementally over time, through selective progressive revelation. Abraham would actually never see much of it even remotely fulfilled during his lifetime. But he believed it by faith, trusting God the whole time, even knowing that much of the promise would be fulfilled in the life to come (Heb 11:13-16). Despite the cryptic nature of the second part of verse three in Genesis 12, God clearly explains the fullness of its meaning through the rest of the Old Testament, the ministry of Jesus and from the New Testament.

The Role of Abraham

When God said He would bless the world "through" him it means that Abraham would be an agent, conduit, channel or vessel of blessing. God would bless the world through those who would come from the loins of Abraham—his offspring, which includes his descendants; namely, the nation of Israel and ultimately the Messiah, who came from the nation of Israel.

Today it is not uncommon for religious scholars to say, "The three greatest religions of the world—Judaism, Christianity and Islam—share the same progenitor in Abraham; he is the patriarch of all three. All three faiths have a common origin. All three faiths can claim allegiance to the promise of Genesis 12:3." On the surface that seems true, but in reality it is historically inaccurate. The promise of Genesis 12:3, whereby God would bless "all the families of the earth" through Abraham, has only been fulfilled in Christianity.

The nation of Israel and Jesus of Nazareth are the specific fulfillments to this promise. Islam categorically rejects Israel and Jesus, as well as the Old Testament as it is written. Non-Christian, unbelieving Judaism rejects Jesus Christ. Neither Islam nor Judaism are real offspring or descendants of Abraham and are therefore foreigners to God's promise as given in the Abrahamic Covenant. As a result, Islam and Judaism have supplanted the true Abrahamic Covenant with deceptive counterfeits. Islam has set aside the Bible, condemning it as a distortion of the truth and they replaced it with their nefarious Koran. Judaism has smothered out the true meaning of the Old Testament, including Genesis 12, with their man-made oral traditions and their Rabbinic writings that obfuscate God's Word as it was originally intended. This was true even in Jesus' day when He confronted His biggest critics, the unbelieving Jewish religious leaders, who claimed to have the corner on the truth when it came to Hebrew Scripture. Jesus exposed them publicly, saying, "Neglecting the commandment of God, you hold to the tradition of men....thus invalidating the word of God by your tradition which you have handed down" (Mark 7:8, 13).

The ultimate goal God had in mind when He said "in you all the families of the earth would be blessed" was simply a worldwide blessing. God would bless the world, but in the proper order: God would first bless the nation of Israel, who came from the loins of Abraham, and then Israel would become a channel of blessing to the nations. God blessing the nation of Israel and preparing them to be a channel of blessing to the world is the story of the Old Testament. God blessing the "families of the earth," or the nations (i.e., Gentiles), through Israel is the story of the New Testament.

God Used Israel

God applies this promise to the nation of Israel when God calls Moses to deliver His people: "I am the God of your father, the God of Abraham....I have surely seen the affliction of My people who are in Egypt, and have given heed to their cry...I have come down to deliver them from the power of the Egyptians, and to bring them up from that land to a good and spacious land, to a land flowing with milk and honey" (Exod 3:6-8). Further, as God established Israel in the land, He calls them to be a priestly nation, charged with the task of proclaiming His excellencies to all surrounding nations (Exod 19:6). He did miracles on behalf of Israel to proclaim His name in all the earth (Exod 9:16). God never intended Israel to be an island unto themselves. They were to be a channel of His blessings, not a self-feeding *cul-de-sac*. Israel, the blessed nation, was to "Tell of His glory among the nations, His wonderful deeds among all the peoples" (Ps 96:3).

Looking back over history, particularly biblical history, Israel has proved to be a blessing to the world in specific ways, thus fulfilling God's intention in this promise. Israel had many faults as a nation and people from the time of Jacob' twelve sons (1850 BC) until the close of the Old Testament (400 BC). Jeremiah, speaking for God, sums up their compromised history: "'Surely, as a woman treacherously departs from her lover, so you have dealt treacherously with Me, O house of Israel,' declares the LORD" (Jer 3:20). Nevertheless, God would use Israel to bless the whole world despite her flaws. God can draw a straight line with a crooked stick, and He did so with Israel.

Special Revelation

The main way God used the sons of Abraham to bless all the families of the earth was through spiritual blessings. There were two primary ones: special revelation and the Messiah, the Savior of the world (John 4:42). Special revelation is divine revelation—the Word of God to man. This is truth about God and reality that comes outside of humanity; it's extrinsic to man's nature, the world and human reason. Special revelation is truth that God makes known by direct revelation, always at His initiative. In history God gave special revelation by speaking through angels, visions, dreams, His prophets and on very rare occasions, audibly. God gave special revelation rarely and selectively. Even more rarely did He command for His special revelation to be written down and preserved permanently.

For the first 2,000 years of world history (from Adam to Abram) there were no permanent written Scriptures. With the exception of Job, it was not until the days of Moses (1400 BC) that God began having His prophets inscripturate His truth. Moses wrote the first five books of the Bible! Then God had many other of His prophets write down permanent Scripture, from Joshua (1350 BC) down to Nehemiah and Malachi (400 BC), and that is how we got the Old Testament. Moses was an Israelite and descendant of Abraham. Moses blessed all the families of the earth by giving us the Pentateuch in written form. Joshua and all the Old Testament prophets were Israelite offspring of Abraham, and what they wrote has been a blessing to the whole world.

Moving from 400 BC to the first century AD, God continued to use Israel to bless the whole world with written revelation. The New Testament was written from about AD 45 (James and Matthew) until the last book of Revelation in about AD 95. Most of the 27 books of the New Testament came from the pen, and ministry, of Israelite, or Hebrew, apostles and prophets. Jesus—the greatest Jew—commissioned His apostles to write the New Testament. The New Testament is all about Israel and Israel's Messiah, Jesus.[25] The New Testament and the Old Testament comprise the Bible, the greatest book ever written. It is the most widely

---

[25] The first Gospel, Matthew, was written by a Jew to a Jewish audience. The Book of James and the Book of Hebrews were written to Jews.

read, most widely distributed, most widely preserved, most widely influential book in history. The Bible, all sixty-six books, is the very Word of God (2 Tim 3:16). The words of Scripture are God's thoughts permanently frozen onto the written page. The truth of the Bible has impacted and blessed all people groups from every corner of the globe. Truly, all the families of the earth have been blessed by the Holy Bible which came from the prophets of Israel. No other written book even comes close to its impact and import. As a matter of fact, all other religious books that have ever been penned pale in comparison and are miserable counterfeits of truth. The main point: if it were not for the Jews, you would not have a Bible.

The Messiah

In addition to special revelation, Israel blessed all the families of the earth by the coming of the Messiah, Jesus Christ of Nazareth. Or in other words, Jesus was the promised Messiah who came from the loins of Abraham and His descendants, and is in fact the greatest fulfillment of the Abrahamic Covenant that was given by God in Genesis 12. When God told Abraham, "in you all the families of the earth will be blessed," that was a promise that the Messiah of the world would come from Israel and would lovingly offer Himself as the final sacrifice for sin on behalf of all people groups. He was the Savior for the Jews (Matt 15:24; John 1:11), but also the Savior for Gentiles (Isa 49:6)—for any man, woman or child who would come to Him as the Lord, pleading for forgiveness of sin (Rom 1:16; Gal 3:28). The Samaritans in Jesus' day came to realize and said of Jesus: "this is indeed the Savior of the world" (John 4:42).

That Jesus was the ultimate fulfillment of the Abrahamic

Covenant as prophesied in Genesis 12 is made clear by Paul in Galatians. Paul quotes Genesis 12:3 and calls it "the gospel." Paul writes,

> The Scripture, foreseeing that God would justify the Gentiles by faith, preached the gospel beforehand to Abraham, *saying*, "All the nations will be blessed in you." So then those who are of faith are blessed with Abraham, the believer (Gal 3:8-9).

This is extraordinary. Paul means something specific when he uses the word "gospel." He means by it the specific content of the message that needs to be proclaimed to sinners so that they might be saved from their sin and God's wrath by being justified, forgiven and given eternal life. The content of this message is the historical reality that Jesus died on the cross for sins according to the Scriptures, and that He was buried and rose again from the dead according to the Scriptures (1 Cor 15:3-4).

The word "gospel" means "good news." The good news is that God has provided a solution to the bad news that sin created—conscious separation from and eternal punishment by a holy God. Jesus, the God-Man, willingly died as a substitute for sinners on the cross to absorb the full wrath of God the Father that was meant for sinners. He guaranteed the salvation of repentant and believing sinners by rising from the dead and ascending into heaven. There He remains at the right hand of the Father, in the presence of a myriad of angels and all the past saints of history, as High Priest and Head of the Church. He will return physically in glory to glorify His people, judge His enemies, and rule over the earth until He conquers every last enemy, including Satan and death itself (1 Cor 15:25-28). Then He will deliver all things up to the Father for all eternity. This is surely good news. And all that was wrapped up in God's infinite mind when He made the promise to Abraham in Genesis 12.

The main point: if it were not for the nation of Israel, there would not be a Savior for the world, who is Jesus of Nazareth. And without the blessed Savior, every person in history would be eternally doomed. God has indeed blessed the families of the earth through Abraham and his offspring.[26]

Summary

It is the greatest irony that so many in the world today consider Israel and the Jews to be a despicable blemish on humanity when God said just the opposite in Genesis 12— God will bless the world through Abraham and the nation of Israel. The world has indeed been richly blessed by the nation of Israel. Through the nation of Israel God gave the prophets to the world. Through Israel He gave us special revelation, including Holy Scripture, the Bible, the very Word of God, written and compiled by individual Jews over centuries. Through Israel God blessed the world with Jesus the Messiah, the only Savior for the World. And through Israel

---

[26]Mathews aptly summarizes the clear testimony of Genesis that God intends to bless all the nations of the world, but that specific blessing comes only through the line of Israel as God's special people: "The Old Testament consistently portrays God as a universal God who rules the affairs of all the nations, but this does not suggest that God is an international deity worshiped by many names. The distinctive Sinai covenant Israel enjoyed was not shared by others, and it was the necessary vehicle by which the Gentiles must recognize the Lord for salvation. Yahweh was not the God of Moab or Egypt, for instance. Only through God's revelation of himself to Israel would the world of nations have access to salvation. Thus, because of the unity and sole rule of God (cf. Israel's *shema*, Deut 6:4), Paul could speak of God as the 'God of the Gentiles' too, who holds all people accountable for their sins. Salvation comes to us, whether Jew or Gentile, by the one means of faith in the atoning sacrifice of Israel's Greater David, Jesus Christ (Rom 3:27-31; cf. 1 John 2:2)"; Kenneth A. Mathews, *The New American Commentary: Genesis 1-11:26* (USA: Broadman & Holman Publishers, 1996), 429.

God gave the world the gospel, the good news, the only hope for humanity.

6

God Gave Israel the Promised Land

It was noted in chapter one that Genesis 12 was merely the introduction to the details pertaining to the Abrahamic Covenant. The rest of the Bible fills in many more important details. That's what this chapter will highlight, beginning with more promises God gave after Genesis 12:1-3.

The first item to consider as God expands the details of fulfilling the promises of the Abrahamic Covenant pertains to the land. Sandwiched in between the promises of God making Abram a great nation, making his name great, blessing him, and blessing all the families of the earth through him are two references to the Promised Land which God commits to Abraham and his descendants: "Go…to the land which I will show you" (12:1) and "To your descendants I will give this land" (12:7). God's promise to give Israel the land are the bookends of the Abrahamic Covenant, and thus the promise of the land is foundational and core to the Abrahamic Covenant.

God specified which land He was talking about, for it was where the Canaanites were residing, "the land of Canaan" (Gen 12:5-6).[27]

Abram was 75 years old when God first made the land promise to Abram. God repeated His promise to give Israel the land all throughout Old Testament history. Consider just a sampling:

A little later after Abraham and Lot could no longer share the same space God rehearsed His land promise to Abraham: "for all the land which you see, I will give it to you and to your descendants forever" (Gen 13:15). And again God said, "Arise, walk about the land through its length and breadth; for I will give it to you" (13:17).

A few years later, when Abraham was in his eighties God said, "I am the LORD who brought you from Ur of the Chaldeans to give you this land to possess" (Gen 15:7).

When Abraham was nearing ninety God promised, "to you and your future offspring I will give the land where you are residing—all the land of Canaan—as a permanent possession, and I will be their God" (Gen 17:8).

At least five decades later when Abraham was near 140 years old, or older, Abraham told his servant, "The LORD, the God of heaven...swore to me... 'To your descendants I will give this land'" (Gen 24:7).

---

27 Walt Kaiser notes, "In the Old Testament, the land...is mentioned more than 1,000 times. Two hundred of these references are directly to Israel and appear some 70 times in the book of Deuteronomy alone. As the Old Testament scholar Gerhard Von Rad summarized it, 'Of all the promises made to the Patriarchs it was that of the land that was most prominent and decisive.' To put it another way, the Old Testament theme of the land is more common than the mention of covenants, which many scholars regard as fundamental to the message of the Bible. In fact, the term 'land' that many readers of the Bible assume is a nonessential detail is one of the central aspects of the covenant"; *What Should We Think About Israel?* ed. J. Randall Price (Eugene, OR: Harvest House Publishers, 2019), 70.

After Abraham dies God appeared to Isaac and said, "Sojourn in this land and I will be with you and bless you, for to you and to your descendants I will give all these lands, and I will establish the oath which I swore to your father Abraham....I will give your descendants all these lands" (Gen 26:3-4).

Isaac later blesses his son Jacob, reminding him of the Abrahamic Covenant land promise: "May He also give you the blessing of Abraham, to you and your descendants with you; that you may possess the land of your sojournings, which God gave to Abraham" (Gen 28:4).

About the same time, just before Jacob found a wife, God spoke to him in a dream and said, "I am the LORD, the God of your father Abraham and the God of Isaac; the land on which you lie, I will give it to you and to your descendants" (28:13).

More than twenty years later God appeared to Jacob again at Bethel in Canaan and said to him, "the land which I gave to Abraham and Isaac, I will give it to you, and I will give the land to your descendants after you" (Gen 35:12).

When Jacob was near death at age 147, he blessed his son Joseph saying God "will give this land to your descendants after you for an everlasting possession" (Gen 48:4).

Upon his deathbed Jacob, who had become Israel, prophesied and blessed his twelve sons who would be the direct progenitors of the nation of Israel. Among the promises Israel made to his sons, several pertain to the future land they would inherit. To Judah Jacob promised, "The scepter shall not depart from Judah, nor the ruler's staff from between his feet, until Shiloh comes, and to him shall be the obedience of the peoples" (Gen 49:10). This was a promise that Israel would possess Judah, the capital of Israel, until all the prophecies of the Messiah should be fulfilled. Many of those prophesies are yet to come. God promised Zebulun the land by "the seashore...toward Sidon," the land between the Sea of Galilee and the Mediterranean (Gen 49:13), an area where Jesus had a prominent ministry. Jacob promised Levi, the priestly line, that his descendants would be dispersed throughout the land of Israel (49:7). God fulfilled this prophesy literally 400 years later (around 1390 BC) when Joshua allocated 48 cities to Levi all throughout the Promised Land, ten of which were east of the Jordan (Josh 21). To Issachar Jacob promised the land that was a "good resting place" where "the land was pleasant" (Gen 49:15) which specifically referred to the fertile area between the eastern Jezreel Valley and the Jordan Valley (Josh 19:17-23), just south of the Sea of Galilee.

In the 1400's BC, when Moses was about 80 (Acts 7:23, 30), God appeared to him promising to deliver His people, Israel, from slavery in Egypt "to bring them up from that land to a good land and spacious land, to a land flowing with milk and honey, to the place of the Canaanite...I will bring you up out of the affliction of Egypt to the land of the Canaanite" (Exod 3:8, 17).

Soon after God spoke to Moses again saying, "I am the LORD; and I appeared to Abraham, Isaac and Jacob, as God Almighty...and I also established My covenant with them, to give them the land of Canaan...say, therefore, to the sons of Israel..., 'I will bring you to the land which I swore to give to Abraham, Isaac, and Jacob, and I will give it to you for a possession; I am the LORD'" (Exod 6:4, 8).

When God was about to deliver Israel from Egypt with the tenth plague of death, around 1445 BC, God instituted the Passover, and God commanded His people, "it will come about when you enter the land which the LORD will give you, as He has promised, that you shall observe this rite" (Exod 12:25).

After God delivered Israel from Egypt and brought them through the Red Sea to Mount Sinai in the wilderness, He reminded His people of Commandment number five: "Honor your father and mother so that you may have a long life in the land that the Lord your God is giving you" (Exod 20:12). He further explains how He will enable Israel to possess the hostile land: "For My angel will go before you and bring you to the land of the Amorites, Hethites, Perizzites, Canaanites, Hivites, and Jebusites, and I will wipe them out....I will drive them out little by little ahead of you until you have become numerous and take possession of the land" (Exod 23:23, 30). Then God goes on to delineate the major borders of the Promised Land: "I will set your borders from the Red Sea to the Mediterranean Sea, and from the wilderness to the Euphrates River. For I will place the inhabitants of the land under your control, and you will drive them out ahead of you" (23:31).

While Moses was up on Mount Horeb receiving the Law of God, Aaron and the Israelites made a golden calf and worshipped it. God became angry and wanted to wipe the people out. Moses pleaded with God reminding Him of His covenant promise to Abraham when He promised, "all this land of which I have spoken I will give to your descendants, and they shall inherit it forever" (Exod 32:13). God relented, kept His promise and showed mercy.

Soon after this event God reiterated the promise once more to Moses: "the LORD spoke to Moses, 'Depart, go up from here...to the land of which I swore to Abraham, Isaac, and Jacob, saying, 'To your descendants I will give it'" (Exod 33:1).

In the second year of the Exodus, God spoke to Moses about the land again saying, "You are to possess their land, and I Myself will give it to you to possess it, a land flowing with milk and honey…When you enter the land I am giving you, the land will observe a Sabbath to the LORD" (Lev 20:24; 25:2).

At this same time God reminds Moses and Israel that, as the Creator, He ultimately remained the true owner of the Promised Land, and the whole earth (Ps 24:1); humans are stewards, not owners, of God's precious possession (1 Cor 4:17; Jam 1:17). That was also true of the land which God promised to give Israel, for He declared to Moses and the Jews, "The land, moreover, shall not be sold permanently, for the land is Mine; for you are but aliens and sojourners with Me" (Lev 25:23).

In 1,405 BC, the last year of the Exodus, God spoke to the Israelites saying, "you shall take possession of the land and live in it, for I have given the land to you to possess it. And you shall inherit the land by lot according to your families" (Num 33:53-54).

Several months later, just a few weeks before Moses' death, God spoke to the Israelites as they were on the brink of the Promised Land: "See, I have placed the land before you; go in and possess the land which the LORD swore to give to your fathers, to Abraham, to Isaac, and to Jacob, to them and their descendants after them" (Deut 1:8).

At this time, through the prophet Moses, God further informs the Israelites on the extent and duration of the land promise He gave to the nation of Israel: "So you shall keep His statutes and His commandments which I am giving you today, that it may go well with you and with your children after you, and that you may live long on the land which the Lord your God is giving you for all time" (Deut 4:40).

To Joshua, God said, "Be strong and courageous, for you shall give this people possession of the land which I swore to their fathers to give them" (Josh 1:6).

In about 1,000 BC King Solomon prayed with the Israelites about "the land which Thou didst give to their fathers" (1 Kings 8:34).

Psalm 105 renders a poetic expression of the importance of the land promise at the heart of the Abrahamic Covenant:

> He has remembered His covenant forever,
>   The word which He commanded to a thousand
> generations,
> The covenant which He made with Abraham,
>   And His oath to Isaac.
> Then He confirmed it to Jacob for a statute,
>   To Israel as an everlasting covenant,
> Saying, "To you I will give the land of Canaan as the portion
> of your inheritance"
> (105:8-11).

In about 445 BC the leading Levites, along with the Israelites who had returned to the Promised Land after the Babylonian captivity, spoke of God's promise to Abram, "to make a covenant with him, to give him the land of the Canaanite...to give it to his descendants" (Neh 9:8).

There are many more examples, but the above twenty-five instances clearly illustrate that the promise regarding the land was at the heart of the Abrahamic Covenant. And from a survey of the above promises about the land there are several key truths that surface. First, God owns the land and He has the right to give it to whomever He chooses.

Second, God says repeatedly that He gave the land to Israel as their possession.

Third, God gave the land to Israel because He had a special relationship with them—they were His people. God "swore an oath" to the first Jew, Abraham, promising to give him and his descendants the land as one of the ways He chose to bless them. God cannot lie. God always keeps His promises. Paul spends three chapters in Romans (9-11) discussing God's faithfulness to ethnic Israel and the promises He made to the Jews manifest in the covenants and concludes by saying, "the gifts and the calling of God are irrevocable" (Rom 11:29).

Fourth, God gave the land to Israel "forever," as a "permanent" and "everlasting possession," "for all time" and unto "a thousand generations." At no time in the Bible does God ever revoke His promise of giving the land to Israel forever. The promise still stands.

Fifth, God gives the land to the descendants of Abraham who are ethnic Israelites or Jewish people by blood. The Jews have been around since Abraham the first Jew—that's 4,000 years. They are still here. And God clearly said the land would belong to them perpetually. Nowhere does the Bible say God changed His mind and decided to give the land to the Church.

Sixth, God gave the land to Israel unilaterally. It was solely His prerogative to give them the land. God did not cut a conditional deal with Abram about the land. Actually, when Abram was still an idol-worshiping pagan, God told him, "Go to the land that I will show you...and I will give it to you." In other words, Israel's possession and rights to the land were not contingent upon their worthiness. God initiated the promise of land irrespective of Abraham's desires or status.

Seventh, the land still belongs to Israel even at times when they are vacant from the land or a minority in the land or under the control of another power while in the land. The reason that is so is because God owns the land. It is His eternally and He has decided to give it to Israel. God told Israel ahead of time that if they were disobedient then He would discipline or chasten them by removing them *temporarily* from the land and also at times He would bring enemy neighboring nations in to terrorize Israel for the purpose of spiritual chastisement. Carefully read this detailed prophecy God gave Moses about the land before Israel entered and took possession of it:

> 23And if by these things you are not turned to Me, but act with hostility against Me,24 then I will act with hostility against you; and I, even I, will strike you seven times for your sins.25 I will also bring upon you a sword which will **execute vengeance for the covenant**; and when you gather together into your cities, I will send pestilence among you, so that **you shall be delivered into enemy hands**.26 When I break your staff of bread, ten women will bake your bread in one oven, and they will bring back your bread in rationed amounts, so that you will eat and not be satisfied.
>
> 27Yet if in spite of this you do not obey Me, but act with hostility against Me, 28then I will act with wrathful hostility against you, and I, even I, will punish you seven times for your sins. 29Further, you will eat the flesh of your sons and the flesh of your daughters you will eat. 30I then will destroy your high places, and cut down your incense altars, and heap your remains on the remains of your idols, for My soul shall abhor you. 31I will lay waste your cities as well and will make your sanctuaries desolate, and I will not smell your soothing aromas. 32**I will make the land desolate** so that your enemies who settle in it will be appalled over it. 33You, however, **I will**

71

scatter among the nations and will draw out a sword after you, as your land becomes desolate and your cities become waste (Lev 26:23-33).

Immediately after this sobering threat from God, He then gives them the good news about the land if they repent:

[40]If they confess their iniquity and the iniquity of their forefathers, in their unfaithfulness which they committed against Me, and also in their acting with hostility against Me— [41]I also was acting with hostility against them, to bring them into the land of their enemies—or if their uncircumcised heart becomes humbled so that they then make amends for their iniquity, [42]then **I will remember My covenant with Jacob, and I will remember also My covenant with Isaac, and My covenant with Abraham as well, and I will remember the land.** [43]For the land will be abandoned by them, and will make up for its sabbaths while it is made desolate without them. They, meanwhile, will be making amends for their iniquity, because they rejected My ordinances and their soul abhorred My statutes. [44]Yet in spite of this, when they are in the land of their enemies, I will not reject them, nor will I so abhor them as to destroy them, breaking My covenant with them; for I am the Lord their God. [45]But I will remember for them the covenant with their ancestors, whom I brought out of the land of Egypt in the sight of the nations, that I might be their God. I am the Lord (Lev 26:40-45).

Israel has been chastened many times in the past 4,000 years by God as He has brought in hostile enemies to their land (Lev 26:17), while at other times He has scattered them out of the land (Deut 28:36).[28] He did this, in fulfillment of His

---

[28] Even when they were displaced, scattered abroad and dispersed over the course of centuries, God preserved the Jews' homogeneity as a nation. "There is no parallel in all of human history to the Diaspora ['dispersion'] of the Jews. Here a people scattered across the face of the earth maintained itself for two thousand years without either a homeland or a common language. They maintained their religion, their identity, their separateness,

Word, to refine them, humble them, prune them, and prepare them for the final fulfillment of all the promises He made to them in the Old Testament. In His perfect timing YHWH will bring Israel back to the land, completely, once and for all, as an entire nation, to be His stewards over the Promised Land, where they will enjoy the benefits of the land to its full extent for the first time in history (Deut 30:1-10; Rom 11:25-31).

Summary

At the heart of the Abrahamic Covenant was God's promise to give the land of Canaan to Abraham's descendants. God made this promise to Abraham while he was a pagan. God told Abraham that the promise was forever. God's promise was based on an oath He made. God repeated this promise for 100 years during Abraham's life. God repeated the promise to Isaac, Jacob, Jacob's twelve sons, to Moses over the course of forty years, to Joshua, to Solomon, and to the Levites after the Exile. And God made it clear that even if Israel becomes disobedient, the promise of the land remains, albeit, temporary blessings will be withheld from Israel until they repent. But the promise to the land has never been reneged.

---

and above all, their communal brotherhood—so that a Jew from one community might enter another community in another nation two thousand miles away, yet be immediately accepted and among his own"; Howard Fast, *The Jews: A Story of a People* (New York, NY: Dell Publishing, 1968), 161.

7

Who are the Palestinians?

Who are the Palestinians? The technical answer is different, and very confusing, depending upon what time in history one is referring to. Today the popular notion is that a Palestinian is a non-Jewish Arab who is indigenous to the land of Palestine in the Middle East, such as the late terrorist, Yasser Arafat, or today's terrorist group, Hamas. One hundred years ago a Palestinian could have been a Jew living in Jerusalem. In 1,000 BC a Palestinian was a reference to the Philistines, from Philistia, intruders to Canaan living in the southern coastal plain of Israel on the Mediterranean Sea, like the giant Goliath (1 Sam 17). So, is a Palestinian a modern Arab, a historic Jew or an ancient pagan Philistine? Well, it depends. Houston…we have a problem!

Having an accurate understanding of who the Palestinians really are is critical to having a correct view of Israel today. Unfortunately, historical revisionism has ruled the day on this issue for the past generation—for at least the past five decades in fact. The truth from a popular perspective is distorted, and smothered, beneath layers of false, deep-seated narratives perpetrated by Israel's enemies, including the mainstream media, to a degree that is difficult to override. But this chapter will give it a shot.

Palestine in the Bible

It's easiest to start from the beginning, in Old Testament history, in order to come up with a legitimate definition of "Palestine." Starting with the Bible, it is significant to know that the word "Palestine" is not even in Scripture! At least you will not find that word in the most popular English translations of the Bible, including the NASB, ESV, NIV, NKJV and the CSB. Significantly, and amazingly, the word "Palestine" is never mentioned in the Quran either. Historically, Muslims never considered "Palestine" to be one of their holy sites.

One of the ironies in the Arab-Israeli dispute over "Palestine" is the oft-neglected fact that there is no Palestine in the Muslim or Arab tradition. Neither Filastin (Palestine) nor al-Quds (Jerusalem) is mentioned in the Koran. During more than a millennium when Muslims (both Arabs and Ottoman Turks) ruled the Middle east—from 633 to 1917, with the exception of the century of the Crusaders' reign (1099 to 1187)—there was never a separate entity encompassing the general area of today's Israel/Palestine.[29]

So today, the Jews and the Muslim Arabs are warring over what to do with "Palestine" when that word is not even in either of their most sacred books. How is that possible? That's what we have to untangle—attempting the impossible by unscrewing the inscrutable.

To do this we need to (1) deal with the Bible's treatment of the word Palestine; (2) identify historically who the

---

[29] Craig Parshall, "The Legal Issues at the Nexus of the Conflict," *Israel, the Church and the Middle East*, ed. Bock and Glaser, 207.

Palestinians actually were; (3) explain Rome's use of the word "Palestine" in the second century AD; (4) show how the Brits invoked the word "Palestine" in the early twentieth century; (5) and finally explain how two radical Arabs co-opted the word "Palestine" to suit their terrorist cause since 1967. All these variables contribute to the modern, convoluted portrayal of where Palestine is and what constitutes a true Palestinian.

First is the issue of the Bible's handling of the word "Palestine." Despite what I just said about English Bibles not mentioning the word "Palestine," the King James Bible actually has one occurrence of the word in Joel 3:4, which reads as follows:

> Yea, and what have ye to do with me, O Tyre, and Zidon, and all the coasts of **Palestine**? Will ye render me a recompense? And if ye recompense me, swiftly and speedily will I return your recompense upon your own head.

All other English translations translate "Palestine" as "Philistia" here, which refers to the small region in the south-west coast of Canaan where the Philistine people lived when Abram first entered the Promised Land. "Tyre and Sidon" refer to the coastal district in north-western Canaan and they were the two main cities of Phoenicia. Situated on the Mediterranean seacoast, Sidon was about twenty-five miles north of Tyre. Joel mentions Tyre and Sidon along with the Philistine plain to represent all the western coastland along the Mediterranean. "Palestine" or "Philistia" in Joel's day referred to its five great cities and princes (cf. Josh 13:2). This verse, written by Joel around 900 BC, is actually God warning His enemies and the enemies of Israel, that judgment is coming for the sins of theft and the slave-trade directed at

Israel. Tyre, Sidon and the land of Philistia were known for their seaports on the Great Sea, which is where the slave-trading happened that Joel is condemning. Palestine or Philistia in this context, and throughout the whole Old Testament, is a region composed of only a fraction of all the land of Canaan or Israel. Philistia as a whole was not much bigger than the Dead Sea. So for Joel, "Palestine" does not refer to the entire Promised Land, but only a tiny portion of it. As a matter of fact, Joel distinguishes "Judah" from "Palestine" in 3:1 and even refers to the whole area as "Israel" (3:2), not Palestine. So even the King James Bible never refers to the whole land of Canaan as "Palestine," but only the small lot on the south-west coast; and even then he's talking about the land of the ancient Philistines, not the modern day home of the deceased Yasser Arafat.

Another important note about Joel 3:4—consider how the New American Standard translates it:

> Moreover, what are you to Me, O Tyre, Sidon and all the regions of **Philistia**? Are you rendering Me a recompense? But if you do recompense Me, swiftly and speedily I will return your recompense on your head.

All the other modern English Bibles translate the word "Philistia" in Joel 3:4 as the NASB does and not as the KJV did when it rendered a specific Hebrew word such as "Palestine." That Hebrew noun used is *Palashet* and occurs eight times in the Old Testament. For whatever reason the King James translators back in 1611 did not translate the proper noun *Palashet* the same way in all eight usages. Actually, they translated it four different ways: Palestine, Palestina, Philistia and Philistines. Here's the King James breakdown in the eight verses:

(Exod 15:14)—The people shall hear, and be afraid: sorrow shall take hold on the inhabitants of **Palestina**/*palashet*.

(Ps 60:8)—Moab is my washpot; over Edom will I cast out my shoe: **Philistia**/*palashet* triumph thou because of me.

(Ps 83:7)—Gebal, and Ammon, and Amalek; the **Philistines**/*palashet* with the inhabitants of Tyre.

(Ps 87:4)—I will make mention of Rahab and Babylon to them that know me: behold **Philistia**/*palashet* and Tyre, with Ethiopia; this man was born there.

(Ps 108:9)—Moab is my washpot; over Edom will I cast out my shoe; over **Philistia**/*palashet* will I triumph.

(Isa 14:29, 31)—Rejoice not thou, whole **Palestina**/*palashet*, because the rod of him that smote thee is broken…Howl, O gate; cry; O city; thou, whole **Palestina**/*palashet*, art dissolved.…

(Joel 3:4)—Yea, and what have ye to do with me, O Tyre, and Zidon, and all the coasts of **Palestine**/*palashet*? Will ye render me a recompense? And if ye recompense me, swiftly and speedily will I return your recompense upon your own head.

The Hebrew noun, *palashet*, should never have been translated as "Palestine," but rather as "Philistia," which is what the NASB has done in all eight cases.[30] The Hebrew noun *palashet*, from the verb root, *palash*, means "to roll (in dust; migratory)" and most basically refers to "a territory on the southern Mediterranean coast of Israel"; "a region of Syria." The origin and significance of the word "Philistia" is

---

[30] *The New BDBG Hebrew and English Lexicon with an Appendix Containing the Biblical Aramaic*, ed. Francis Brown, S. R. Driver and Charles Briggs (Peabody, Massachusetts: Hendrickson Publishers, 1979), 814.

unknown,[31] but in the Old Testament it is used in reference to a geographical area, which was the area occupied by the Philistines, the perennial enemy of Israel from the days of Abraham (2000 BC; Gen 21:34) until the days of Jeremiah (600 BC; Jer 47:1).[32]

Our word "Palestine" actually comes from the word "Philistine."[33] So technically, historically, and according to the Bible, the Palestinians are the Philistines. But no one uses the word Palestinian that way today, for a lot of reasons. The most obvious is the fact that they were obliterated before the 6th century BC. It wasn't until the 5th century BC that Herodotus and other classical writers first used the word "Palestine" as a designation for southern Syria, the region north of Egypt, which the Bible called "Canaan."[34]

---

31 Edward M. Blaiklock, "Palestine" (Douglas/Tenney), 742; Although, one source argues, "The Hebrew word *palash* probably comes from the Ethiopic root *palasa*, 'to wander,' or 'emigrate,' and hence *palashat* will signify 'the nation of emigrants'—the Philistines (q. v.) having emigrated from Africa...The people gave their name to the territory in which they settled on the south-west coast of Palestine"; "Palestine," *Cyclopedia of Biblical, Theological, and Ecclesiastical Literature: Volume VII* (New-Pes, 1981), 554.

32 J. C. Moyer, "Since there is no good Sem. etymology for the word, it may be of Indo-European origin," 767, *The Zondervan Pictorial Encyclopedia of the Bible: Vol. 4*, "Philistines", ed. Merrill Tenney (Grand Rapids, MI: Zondervan, 1976), 767.

33 John B. Graybill, "Philistines," *The New International Dictionary*, ed. Douglas and Tenney, 782.

34 "The name 'Palestine' was originally an adjective derived from Heb....*Peleshet*. It is first mentioned in Herodotus in the form of...'the Philistine Syria'; subsequently, the name was shortened and the adjective 'Palaistinei' became a proper noun. Philo identifies 'Palaistinei' with biblical Canaan. In Talmudic literature Palestine is used as the name of a Roman province, adjoining the provinces of *Finukyah* (Phoenicia) and *Aruvyah* (Arabia; Gen. R. 90:6). From the fourth century, however, the three provinces into which the Land of Israel was divided were referred to as the 'first,' 'second,' and 'third Palestine' respectively. The Arabs used the term 'Filastin'...for the 'first Palestine' only, differentiating between it and 'Urdunn'... (Jordan); but these designations soon fell into disuse, as the

Prior to that time Palestine, or Philistia, was restricted to a smaller area on the Eastern Mediterranean Sea extending from Gaza going north to Joppa.[35] This was the area that God had allocated to Dan and Judah in the days of Joshua (Judges 1:18-19). The tribe of Dan failed to conquer their designated area by the sea that was occupied by the Philistines (Judges 18:1) so they were forced north and eventually conquered Leshem (Laish of Judges 18:29) and renamed it Dan (Joshua 19:47; Judges 18:1-29). Not displacing the evil Philistines was a lack of faithfulness and courage on the part of Dan and as a result the Philistines would prove to be a scourge to the nation of Israel for the next 700 years!

According to the Bible, all the area west of the Jordan river up to the Mediterranean Sea was known as Canaan before God led Israel there through Joshua (around 1400 BC). This area was a strategic land bridge connecting Africa and Asia. It was prime real estate.

This territory was situated between the great ancient

Araba generally referred to provinces by the names of their capital cities. The crusaders renewed the use of the 'three Palestines,' the borders of which, however, differed from those of the Roman provinces. After the fall of the crusader kingdom, Palestine was no longer an official designation, but it was still used in non-Jewish languages as the name of the 'Holy Land' on both sides of the Jordan. It was not an administrative unit under the Ottoman Empire, when it was part of the province of Syria." Abraham J. Brawer, "Palestine," *Encyclopedia Judaica: Volume 13, P-Rec* (Jerusalem, Israel: Keter Publishing House, 1971), 30; see also Grayzel, who simply notes, "The Greeks, who were at that time [450-350 BC] the only people interested in history, philosophy and geography, called the land between the Mediterranean and the Jordan 'Philistina' (Palestine), because the only people they knew in that land were the Philistines who lived on the coast"; Solomon Grayzel, *A History of the Jews: From the Babylonian Exile to the Present* (The Jewish Publication Society of America, 1968), 45.

[35] The Bible clearly gives the boundaries of Philistia which included five cities: Gaza, Ashdod, Ashkelon, Gath and Ekron; cf. Joshua 13:3. The Bible also makes it clear that this area was occupied by the Canaanites before the Philistines came and displaced them.

empires of the Tigris-Euphrates and the Halys rivers on the one hand, and the great Egyptian empire of the Nile on the other. It was providential that the nation Israel, with its testimony to the knowledge of the one true God and with its obligation to make known that fact, should inherit a country that formed a geographical bridge between the ancient centers of pagan civilization.[36]

Before Canaan became an area of land, Canaan was the name of a real man. He is first mentioned in the Bible right after the Flood not long after Noah exited the ark. Moses informs the reader, "Ham was the father of Canaan" (Gen 9:18), which makes Canaan the grandson of Noah. Noah's son, Ham, violated Noah in some unspeakably immoral manner, and as a result, God did not just punish Ham, He cursed Ham's entire lineage beginning with his son Canaan (9:25). As a result, the offspring of Canaan would become a corrupt, immoral, compromised, wicked people, polluting the land and everyone around them. God, therefore, sovereignly chose to expunge them from the land. The Canaanites were so vile and their reputation so wicked that the word "Canaanite" became a metaphorical and proverbial term or derision to describe that which was immoral, degenerate and unholy (Zech 14:21).

Canaan is next mentioned in Genesis 10 where Moses describes how Canaan the man has descendants and thus becomes Canaan the people-group and a confederation of nation-states (Josh 3:10), around 2500 BC:

> The sons of Ham were Cush and Mizraim and Put and Canaan....Canaan became the father of Sidon, his firstborn, and Heth and the Jebusite and the Amorite and the Girgashite

---

36 Merrill F. Unger, "Canaan," *The New Unger's Bible Dictionary*, ed. R. K. Harrison (Chicago: Moody Press, 1988), 202.

and the Hivite and the Arkite and the Sinite and the Arvadite and the Zemarite and the Hamathite; and afterward the families of the Canaanite were spread abroad. The territory of the Canaanite extended from Sidon as you go toward Gerar, as far as Gaza; as you go toward Sodom and Gomorrah and Admah and Zeboiim, as far as Lasha. These are the sons of Ham, according to their families, according to their languages, by their lands, by their nations (Gen 10:6, 15-20).

This passage clearly delineates the boundaries of what would become the "Promised Land," or "land of promise" (Heb 11:9), that God would give to Israel. "Sidon" marks the northern-most coastal town. The western border was the Mediterranean "as you go toward Gerar." "Gerar" marks the southern border and the four cities, Sodom, Gomorrah, Admah and Zeboiim mark the southeasterly border of Canaan.[37]

Beginning in Genesis 10, when all nations first began, this land is known as "the land of Canaan," not Palestine! To call this land "Palestine" is to invoke a true and significant anachronism, an illegitimate back-reading of later history into a time-period when such a name did not exist, nor did it correspond to the land area at hand. In 2100 BC that area was called "the land of Canaan" before Abram arrived there (Gen 11:31; 12:5). When Abram arrived and ventured all throughout the region, "the Canaanites were in the land" (Gen 12:6). All throughout Genesis it is called "the land of Canaan," forty times, from the time of Abram until the days of Joseph (1800 BC). God promised to give the Jews the land

---

[37] This passage does not exhaust the boundaries of the land God promised Abraham for Genesis 15:18-21 and Deuteronomy 1:7 describe the land as far east as the Euphrates. In addition, "The boundaries of Canaan as defined in Num 34 and in Egyptian texts take in Phoenician coastline (modern Lebanon) as well as southwest Syria"; Gordon J. Wenham, *Word Biblical Commentary: Genesis 1-15* (Nashville: Thomas Nelson, 1987), 224.

of Canaan, not the land of Palestine. God clearly told Moses, "I also established My covenant with them [Israel], to give them the land of Canaan" (Exod 6:4).

God Himself would lead the Jews into the land as He also would drive out the Canaanites ahead of them: "Driving out the Canaanites...I will send an angel before you" (Exod 33:2). After taking possession of the land under the leadership of Joshua "the land of Canaan" became the property and stewardship of Israel: "Now these are the territories which the sons of Israel inherited in the land of Canaan" (Joshua 14:1). So all the land of Canaan became the land of the twelve tribes of Israel. After Joshua possessed the land God had given him, Scripture begins to refer to that region as Israel's possession in various forms such as "the hill country of Israel" (Joshua 11:16), "the land of the sons of Israel" (11:22), "the land of Israel's inheritance" (Judges 20:6), "the land of Israel" (1 Sam 13:19), "the territory of Israel" (1 Sam 27:1), "the land which I [YHWH] have given them" (1 Kings 9:7), "their land" (Jer 12:4). God Himself calls it "the holy land" and it, along with Jerusalem, belongs to Judah (i.e., "the Jews"; Zech 2:12). Even after the kingdom divided into north and south around 931 BC after the rule of Solomon, the north was known as "Israel" and "Samaria" (1 Kings 16:29) while the south was designated "Judah" (1 Kings 14:21)... never "Palestine" nor "Philistia" nor any other non-Jewish appellation.

God could give Israel the land because He created and owned it. It is called "YHWH'S land" in Hosea 9:3! He also created Israel, elected them as His own and called His very name "the LORD God of Israel" (Jer 34:13). No other nation or land in human history has been given such personalized divine attributions. The point is simple. From the time nations began, the Bible calls the Promised Land "the land of Canaan" until the days of Joshua around 1390 BC when that region took on the designation "the land of Israel." The Bible never calls it Palestine.

Who were the Philistines?

Who were the Philistines? Simply put, the Philistines were the ancient and original Palestinians...and they have no relation to modern-day Islamic Arab Palestinians. They first appear in Genesis in the days of Abram and prove to be a perennial nemesis to Israel until after the 6th century BC when they fade from the annals of history. As a people, the Bible calls them "uncircumcised" (Judges 15:18; 1 Sam 17:26; 1 Chron 10:4), a term of derision, a dirty people, in contrast to Israel, God's special set-apart (i.e., "holy"), circumcised elect nation.

Before occupying the small patch of land on the coast of south-west Canaan, the Philistines inhabited Crete and other regions north of Egypt. They were known as the "Sea people," for they were part of a massive contingent of sea people who invaded Egypt by way of the Aegean Sea around the 13th century BC.

The primary evidence for this comes from the Bible, Egyptian records, and archeological finds. According to the Bible, the Philistines came from Caphtor (Jer 47:4; Amos 9:7; cf. Gen 10:14; Deut 2:23; 1 Chron 1:12) which is generally thought to be Crete. The Cretan origin is supported by the term "Cherethites," a name probably meaning "Cretans" and used in reference to the Philistines or a part of them. First Samuel 30:14 refers to part of the Philistine coast as the "Negeb of the Cherethites." In Ezekiel 25:16 and Zephaniah 2:5 the Philistines and the Cherethites are used in parallelism. Elsewhere, the Cherethites are part of David's personal bodyguard (2 Sam 15:18, etc.) and probably were recruited from the Philistines while David was at Ziklag. Egyptian records refer to a nebulous group of "Sea People" who were invaders coming from the islands in the North. These "Sea People" caused a tremendous upheaval in the ancient Near East at the end of the Late Bronze Age (c. 1200 B.C.).[38]

The Philistines are first mentioned in the Bible in Genesis 10:14 in the Table of Nations as being the descendants of two people groups called the "Pathrusim and Casluhim." These folks were sea people and invaded Egypt in waves, from 2400 BC and again in a significant way in 1200 BC.[39] Egypt successfully repelled them and pushed them north, up toward Canaan, and as a result they end up on the south-western coast of the Promised Land (and later even in the foothills of the tribe of Judah), where they are routinely featured in Scripture as they interface with various Jews, from Abram to the Judges. As a people group, they appear in the Bible in four different time-periods of Israel's history: first with Abraham and his immediate offspring (2100-1900 BC); next during the time of the Exodus and the Judges (1400-1300 BC); then during the reigns of Saul and David (1050-1000 BC); and finally, during the divided monarchy (950-500 BC).

Abraham had an encounter with the Philistines when he was about 100 years old as he ventured into "the land of the Philistines" in southern Canaan in the City of Gerar. Upon entering the city, Abimelech, the king of Gerar, stole Sarah from Abraham and took her as his own. God appeared to the king in a dream and warned him not to touch Sarah, "for she is married" (Gen 20:3). God struck the king's household with a curse and as a result, Abimelech repented and returned

---

38 J. C. Moyer, *Zondervan Pictorial Encyclopedia*, ed. Tenney, 767.
39 Mathews, *Genesis 1-11:26*, 452-455.

Sarah and told Abraham to roam freely throughout the land of Gerar. God responded to Abimelech in grace, healing him and his whole family.

About ninety years later, after Abraham had died, his son Isaac took his family south during a famine to live in the Philistine city of Gerar, the same town Abraham had visited. While there, Abimelech (a title like the Egyptian "Pharaoh") inquired about Isaac's wife, Rebekah, who was beautiful. Isaac lied to the king of Gerar, saying "She is my sister" (Gen 26:7). Abimelech confronted Isaac, who finally confessed to the truth. The king then allowed Isaac to live in the land of the Philistines and God blessed him during his sojourn there, for over time he accumulated "possessions of flocks and herds and a great household, so that the Philistines envied him" (Gen 26:14). Eventually Abimelech, Philistine king of Gerar became threatened by the prosperous Jew and said to Isaac, "Go away from us, for you are too powerful for us" (vs. 16).

These two accounts illustrate that Israel's initial interactions with the Philistines on the southern coast were tolerable—as long as each group stayed clear of the other. They were able to co-exist under certain conditions and agreements. In the future, this would not be the case as the Philistines would grow more aggressive and hostile to Israel, the people of God.

Over the next six centuries the Philistines became more settled, populous, and territorial along the southern coast of the Great Sea. They developed a reputation of being so hostile that in 1440 BC God warned Moses about them and told the Israelite deliverer to lead the Jews out of Egypt by the longer route via the Red Sea as opposed to the short-cut straight up the coast along the Mediterranean in order to avoid the bellicose Philistines:

Now when Pharaoh had let the people go, God did not lead them by way of the land of the Philistines, even though it was near; for God said, "The people might change their minds when they see war and return to Egypt." Hence God led the people around by the way of the wilderness to the Red Sea; and the sons of Israel went up in martial array from the land of Egypt" (Exod 13:17-18).

Joshua had limited interaction with the Philistines as he led Israel into the Promised Land, one tribe at a time. Main resistance from the Philistines came in the region allocated to Dan, who failed to dispel the Philistines. As a result, instead of being purged completely, the Philistines maintained a root in the land of Israel that would bear bitter fruit for the Jews for generations to come (Judges 3:1-3). During the days of the Judges, Israel even adopted the false gods (i.e., Dagon, Ashtoreh, Baalzebub) of the pagan Philistines, thus "they forsook the LORD and did not serve Him" (Judges 10:6). During the entire era of the Israelite Judges, the Philistines consistently pressed inland from the coast harassing Israel. The most formidable campaign against the Philistines was led by Samson (Judges 13-15). But ironically, he could not escape the temptation of their vices as he even married a Philistine woman, and later was betrayed by Delilah, the infamous dame who had Philistine associations. Eventually Samson was taken prisoner by them, having his eyes gouged out, chained to pillars and publicly humiliated as sport before a crowd of thousands. Samson invoked the power of God in one last burst of strength as he toppled the entire massive edifice upon himself and all present as he shouted, "Let me die with the Philistines!" (Judges 16:30).

The Philistines were an advanced people for their time,

particularly in the area of metallurgy, a skill they acquired from other Sea Peoples such as the Hittites those from Antolia,[40] and possibly from the indigenous Canaanites as well (Josh 17:16). As such, the Philistines for a time had a monopoly on iron weapons and tools, including spears and even chariots (1 Sam 13:5, 19-23). This put the Israelites at a disadvantage. It was during the days of Samuel that the Philistines began to flex their military might, wielding their progressive weapons of war, with their sights homed in on the less sophisticated Jews. It was during this period (c. 1070 BC) when the Philistines successfully stole the ark of the covenant from Israel for seven months (1 Sam 4-6). It was also at this time that God raised up King Saul to defend Israel, as he would kill his thousands in war, and King David who would slaughter tens of thousands, many of those enemies being the pesky Philistines.

The apex of Philistine hostility toward Israel is poignantly illustrated in the famous battle between David, the Jew, and Goliath, the ten-foot tall Philistine champion, who bore 125-pound armor and wielded a spear with a 15-pound iron tip. Goliath publicly mocked Israel and their God for forty straight days in a valley near Judah, challenging Israel to send forth their best warrior for slaughter. David, who was just a budding lad, the youngest of eight brothers, heard the blasphemous giant's taunts and with disdain asked the fearful, paralyzed Israelite soldiers looking on, "Who is this uncircumcised Philistine, that he should taunt the armies of the living God?" (1 Sam 17:26). Outsized, under-experienced, with no armor, with only five smooth stones and a stick in his

---

[40] Eugene H. Merrill, *The Bible Knowledge Commentary: Old Testament*, "1 Samuel," ed. John F. Walvoord and Roy B. Zuck (USA: Victor Books, 1988), 445.

hand, David propelled a stone into the behemoth's temple, killing him on the spot, all in the name of YHWH, the God of Abraham, Isaac and Jacob. David eventually ascended to the throne in Israel and led one last major conflict against the Philistines. Led by the LORD Himself, David outmaneuvered the Philistines, striking them from the rear, overwhelming them, effectively ending the power of the Philistines as a serious menace to Israel from that day forward (2 Sam 5:22-25).

After David, the Philistines progressively phased out over time. They showed sporadic signs of life during the days of the Kings (2 Chron 11:8; 1 Kings 15:27), even invading Judah in Jehoram's day where the Jews incurred heavy losses (2 Kings 8:22; 2 Chron 21:16-17). The final acts of aggression toward Israel occurred in the days of Ahaz (732-716 BC; Isa 9:8-12) and they are mentioned for the last time in the Bible in Zechariah. Jeremiah 47 is a prophecy from God indicting the Philistines, predicting their utter destruction:

> On account of the day that is coming
> To destroy all the Philistines,
> To cut off from Tyre and Sidon
> Every ally that is left;
> For the LORD is going to destroy the Philistines,
> The remnant of the coastland of Caphtor (Jer 47:4).

Jeremiah predicted that the Philistines would be wiped out imminently. That is exactly what happened. Tiny Philistia was caught in the middle of a Battle between Nebuchadnezzar's Babylon and Egypt's Pharaoh between 609-587 BC. The collateral damage was the obliteration of the Philistines from world history. They became an extinct people. As such, there are no Philistines today.[41]

Palestine in the New Testament

The New Testament does not mention the "Philistines," nor does it speak of the land of "Palestine." In keeping with the Old Testament, the Holy Land was known to Jesus, the Jews of His day, the apostles and the early church simply as the land of Israel. At the time of Christ's birth an angel of God spoke to Joseph, saying, "Get up take the Child and His mother, and go into the land of Israel" (Matt 2:20). The Jews, who lived in the land during the New Testament era, also called their land "Zion," a strictly Jewish, Hebrew and long-standing Old Testament appellation for the Holy Land (2 Sam 5:7; Ps 2:6). When God presented Jesus as the Messiah to the nation of Israel at the Triumphal Entry, He was presented to the people of the land of "Zion" (John 12:15). Southern Israel in Jesus' day was called "Judea," for Jesus was born "in Bethlehem of Judea; for this is what has been written by the prophet" (Matt 2:5). "Judea" is another strictly Jewish designation. "Judea" is the Latin translation for the Hebrew "Judah," Judah being the name of one of Jacob's sons who inherited a southern portion of the Promised Land in the days of Joshua. Our English word "Jew" comes from the name "Judah," and throughout history the Promised Land was known as the "land of Judah" or the "land of the Jews."[42]

---

[41] J. P. J. Olivier, "Pelisti, peleset," New International Dictionary of Old Testament Theology & Exegesis: Volume 3, ed. Willem A. Van Gemeren (Grand Rapids, MI: Zondervan, 1997), 633.

[42] "The actual name Judea occurs from the Hellenistic period. It is first used by Clearchus, a disciple of Aristotle...[used] to define the area where the Jews of Erez Israel lived. With the direct Roman rule of Erez Israel, which dates from the banishment of Archelaus to Gaul in 6 C. E., a special

Arabs were not known in the land of the Jews at that time. God had given the Promised Land to the descendants of Abraham, the Israelites. Around 63 BC the Promised Land had been enveloped into the Roman Empire and was partitioned into four distinct regions--Galilee, Samaria, Judea and Perea.[43] During this period, even Rome recognized this area as the land of the Jews and granted them conditional autonomy under the supervision of quasi-Jewish high priests such as John Hyrcanus and Herod.

Jesus did prophecy that God would judge unbelieving Israel by chastening them through foreign invaders—the Romans. Jesus came as the promised Messiah to His own people, the Jews. But, for the most part, the entire nation rejected Him (John 1:11). This rejection was no surprise, for it was prophesied centuries before in Scripture (Isa 53; John 12:37-40). For their unbelief God would temporarily displace some of the Jews, in particular the ones in Jerusalem (where the Temple was) from portions of the land God gave to them. Jesus spoke to this at the end of His earthly ministry just prior to His death:

---

governor was appointed over Judea who was given the title procurator and was responsible to the governor of Syria. The procuratorship was confined to Judea until the accession of Agrippa I to the throne in 41. On the resumption of Roman rule after his death in 44 the procurator's rule was extended over the whole of Israel"; *Encyclopedia Judaica: Volume 10, Jes-Lei* (1971, 1973), 403. Despite centuries of disruption from various foreign invaders Judah's identity as a autonomous vassal remained constant all throughout Old Testament history: "Sargon II noted in one inscription that he was the 'subduer' of the country Judah which is far away....This history of vassalship was disturbed on several occasions, but it is noteworthy that none of them resulted in a change of status for Judah." Peter Machinist, "Palestine: Assyrian and Babylonian Administration," *The Anchor Bible Dictionary: Volume 5, O-Sh*, ed. David Noel Freedman (New York, NY: Doubleday, 1992), 74.

[43] Edward M. Blaiklock, "Herod," *New International Dictionary of the Bible*, 434.

When He approached *Jerusalem*, He saw the city and wept over it, saying, "If you had known in this day, even you, the things which make for peace! But now they have been hidden from your eyes. For the days will come upon you when your enemies will throw up a barricade against you, and surround you and hem you in on every side, and they will level you to the ground and your children within you, and they will not leave in you one stone upon another, because you did not recognize the time of your visitation" (Luke 19:41-44).

This prophecy was fulfilled in exact detail when the Roman General Titus crushed Jerusalem in 70 AD.

> He surrounded the city on Apr. 9, cutting off all supplies, and trapping thousands of people who had been in Jerusalem for the Passover and Feast of Unleavened Bread (just completed). The Romans systematically built embankments around the city, gradually starving the city's inhabitants. The Romans held the city in this manner through the summer, defeating various sections of the city one by one. The final overthrow of the city occurred in early Sept....The Romans utterly demolished the city, temple, residences, and people. Men, women, and children were brutally slaughtered by the tens of thousands. The few survivors were carried off to become victims of the Roman circus games and gladiator bouts.[44]

At the apex of the Roman siege many Jews fled north to Galilee and to the hills throughout the land. Even though the capital city of Jerusalem was razed to the ground, the Romans did not eradicate all Jews from the land. As a matter of fact, the Jews remained a majority in the Promised Land even after

---

[44] John MacArthur, *The MacArthur Study Bible: Twentieth-Anniversary Edition*, New King James Version (Nashville, TN: Thomas Nelson, 2017), 1555.

Jerusalem was destroyed and the land was still known as the land of Israel.[45]

A Historic Name Change

The Jews remained steadfast after Jerusalem was demolished in 70 AD by the Romans and proved to be a resilient people once again, as they had been previously, surviving Gentile intrusion and domination in their land from the time of Assyria in 722 BC, the Babylonians in 605 BC, the Medo-Persians[46] in 539 BC and the Greeks in 330 BC. For the ensuing six decades after the massacre of Titus, the Jews regrouped, waited for a changing of the guard, and with time saw a relaxation of the Roman grip on Jerusalem. A renewed Messianic expectation arose and centered around one rising, high profile leader among the Jews, Simon Ben Kozehav, or popularly known as Bar Kochba, or "Son of the Star," as many believed he was the fulfillment of the prophecy in Numbers 24:17 that declared that "a star will come forth out of Jacob" to rescue Israel.

Hadrian was the Roman Emperor (117-138 AD) in the days of Bar Kochba. He was thoroughly pagan and enthusiastically invested in various shrines and temples to the gods, including one to Jupiter in the heart of Jerusalem. The Jews were originally optimistic about Hadrian's rule as they thought him to be tolerant and cosmopolitan. There were rumors that he would restore the ruins of Jerusalem, cultivate Jewish culture and best of all, rebuild the Jewish Temple. The Jews' hopes were dashed when reality struck, as Hadrian

---

45 Steven Charles Ger, *What Should We Think about Israel?: Separating Fact from Fiction in the Middle East*, ed. J. Randall Price (Eugene, OR: Harvest House Publishers, 2019), 49.

46 Even during exile under Medo-Persian domination the Holy Land was known as Israel and Judah; cf. Ezra 5:1.

renamed Jerusalem with a pagan moniker, *Aelia Capitolina* (in deference to Jupiter Capitolinus). The construction he began there was not for a Jewish Temple, but rather a temple to Jupiter in keeping with his cultic bent. This outraged the Jews.

Since the time of the Zealots, there had always been an unbroken line of Jewish nationalism that fed ongoing revolts and rebellions against foreign, Gentile occupiers. Bar Kochba was of such lineage. He would not tolerate pagan desecration of the Holy Land, thus taking it upon himself to lead another revolt against Rome. This came to pass in 132 AD:

Bar Kochba and his rebels surprised the Romans and captured hundreds of cities, towns, and villages, including Jerusalem. They established an independent Jewish government to rule the land they liberated and minted coins proclaiming the "freedom of Jerusalem."[47]

This was no small-time, insignificant localized uprising that could be ignored. On the contrary,

> the insurrection, which was prepared in detail "until the whole of Judea was in revolt" ([meaning]...most of Erez Israel, including Galilee and Golan). He [Dio Cassius, the historian] further states that the Jews "throughout the world" supported the rising as did non-Jews, too, and it was "as though the whole world raged." In its scope and vehemence, the revolt assumed the dimensions of a war which constituted a threat to the empire.[48]

As such, Emperor Hadrian retaliated in a fury. He dispatched an overwhelming military force, led by General Julius Severus who gradually, over the course of three years, quelled the

---

[47]David Brog, *Reclaiming Israel's History* (Washington, DC: Regnery Publishing, 2017), 17.

[48] "Bar Kokhba," *Encyclopedia Judaica: Volume 4, B* (Jerusalem, Israel: Keter Publishing House, 1971, 1973), 234.

revolt with a systematic scorched-earth policy that ended in a wholesale massacre of the Jews, crushing fifty fortresses, destroying 985 Jewish villages, and slaughtering almost 600,000 people in addition to those who died of starvation, disease and fire. In contrast to their attack on Jerusalem in 70 AD that simply ended with the destruction of the city, this time the Romans, compelled by Hadrian, were intent on making a permanent statement in an attempt to ethnically cleanse all things Jewish in the land of Israel, particularly in the vicinity of Judea. All Jews were expelled from city of Jerusalem (Aelia Capitolina)—any who tried to re-enter faced immediate execution.[49] Study of the Torah was banned and a generation of rabbis were executed. Synagogues were destroyed. Almost all of Judea was exterminated of anything Jewish. Jewish land was expropriated. Tax rates on the whole land became exorbitant. The once Holy City, Zion of the Jews, had been summarily made heathen. And in an attempt to permanently eradicate all memory of the Jews and their religion from the land, Hadrian changed the name of the country from "Judea," the land of the Jews, to "Syria Palestine," the land of the "Philistines," derived from the historic and most loathed enemies of the Israelites.[50]

Thenceforth, from 135 AD on, the ill-conceived pseudonym of Palestine, chosen out of sheer malice, would effectively supplant the God-given name of the Promised Land, "Israel," thus effectively blurring the true historical lineage and identity of the land given to Abraham, Isaac and Jacob.[51] As previously, in 70 AD, despite the widespread

---

[49] "Palestine," *The New Unger's Bible Dictionary*, 957.
[50] Brog, *Israel's History*, 18.
[51] "All ancient writers, therefore, did not use the name in the same sense-- some applying it to the whole country of the Jews, some restricting it to Philistia. Consequently, when the name Palestine occurs in classic and

devastation, God's people could not be completely eradicated (Jer 31:35-37), for in the aftermath the Jews still remained a majority in the land with many more fleeing north toward Galilee and into the surrounding hills and distant rural areas.

"Palestine" Through the Centuries (AD 135-1917)

From the time of Hadrian (AD 135) until the first World War (1917), Judea was swallowed up into various empires from the Roman, to the Byzantine, to the Arabs, to the Mamluks, to the Ottoman Turks and finally to the British. During those times it went by various designations, Syria being the most common. Its borders fluctuated from century to century, arbitrarily, often ill-defined and as a consequence the name "Palestine" had virtually no consistent meaning, significance, or even official status until after World War I when the British assumed a mandate over part of the region.

Consequently the name "Palestine" seems over the centuries (with the exception of the period 1920-1948), to have covered either too little or too much to have precise meaning, either it described a part of the larger whole that was Syria, or it covered parts of the political unities formed by adjoining states.[52]

---

early Christian writers, the student of geography will require carefully to examine the context, that he may ascertain whether it is applied to Philistia alone, or to all the land of Israel"; "Palestine," *Cyclopedia of Biblical, Theological, and Ecclesiastical Literature: Volume VII, New-Pes*, ed. John McClintock and James Strong (Grand Rapids, MI: Baker Book House, 1981), 555.

[52] J. H. Paterson, "Palestine," *Zondervan Pictorial Encyclopedia*, 564. Bornemann simplifies the complex when he notes, "The name 'Palestine' is commonly used to designate the ancient land of the Bible, the Holy Land— "from Dan to Beer-Sheba." It is also the common name for the territory of the British mandate taken over by the United Nations in 1948 and held now by the Palestinian Authority and the State of Israel...Originally, however, its boundaries were not so definitely defined, and Palestine was not its name"; Robert Bornemann, "Palestine," *The Encyclopedia of*

The British conquered Palestine from the Ottoman Turks in 1918, formally securing a Mandate for Palestine in 1920 which lasted until 1948. During this period the Brits used the term "Palestine" to designate a region, not a people, religion, ethnicity or nationality. At that time if you lived in "Palestine" you may have been Jewish, a Muslim Arab, a Jewish Arab, a Christian Arab, British, a Syrian Muslim, a Turk, etc. There was no Palestinian language, no Palestinian religion, no Palestinian ethnicity, race or nationality, no Palestinian culture. Palestine was an imprecise, manufactured name, pragmatically utilized and misapplied for convenient political purposes. The Arabs living in the land prior to WWI considered themselves citizens of the Ottoman Empire, or Syrians and Arabs—not Palestinians.[53]

Modern Palestine—1964 to Present Day

The modern popular meaning of "Palestine," "Palestinian" and "The State of Palestine" can be attributed primarily to two radical Arab Muslims: Mohammed Amin al-Husseini (1897-1974) and Yasser Arafat (1929-2004). Today the popular understanding of the word "Palestinian" refers to Muslim Arabs who are first and foremost victims, indigenous to the land formerly known as Canaan. Further, they

---

Christianity: Volume 4, ed. Geoffrey W. Bromiley (Grand Rapids, MI: Eerdmans Publishing Company, 1997), 14.

[53]"As in other parts of the globe they ruled, the European powers carved up the former Ottoman territories with little regard for local loyalties or preferences. The mandates imposed [upon former Syria by France and Great Britain in 1920] created borders—and eventually identities—that had never before existed. Palestine was one of those new creations. While 'Palestine' was a name with profound historic resonance for Europeans, it had no such significance to most of the people who happened to live there. To the extent that the Arabic speakers of Palestine identified with a geographic entity smaller than the Ottoman Empire, it was with Syria. Thus their first response to British efforts to separate them into a new entity called Palestine was to resist them"; Brog, *Israel's History*, 47.

supposedly have been illegitimately forced out of their homeland by occupying, alien invaders, the Jews, who, through violence, have forced the Arabs out of most of the region, leaving them deprived and confined to a mere fraction of the land in the Gaza Strip and the West Bank. This historical fiction is the by-product of a deliberate mis-information campaign begun in the 1920's that culminated in 1974 and is the accepted, entrenched metanarrative of today's pop culture.[54]

Amin al-Husseini was an Arab Muslim born in Jerusalem to a wealthy and politically influential family during the days of the Ottoman Empire. From birth he was reared on Arab nationalism as well as a healthy dose of anti-Semitic propaganda, such as the fabricated 1903 Russian pamphlet, *The Protocols of the Elders of Zion*, that asserted the Jews had a plan to take over the world.[55] In his youth he was a loyal

---

[54] "The efforts of Husseini and Arafat's rebel labors formally came to fruition in 1974 when the Arab League met in Morocco and passed a resolution recognizing a Palestinian right to 'self-determination,' which was followed that same year by UN Resolution 3236, recognizing the existence of the Palestinian people"; Craig Parshall, *Israel and the Church*, 207.

[55] The nefarious impact that *The Protocols* had on galvanizing anti-Semitism among Islamic Arabs in Palestine in the 1920's and 1930's up to the present day cannot be overstated. Although it has been exposed as a pure, fictitious hoax, it has been imbibed into the mainstream Muslim-Arab world as gospel truth and remains one of the basic functional playbooks for modern-day Palestinian Muslim-Arabs of how to regard the "dirty" Jew: "The Protocols of the Elders of Zion codified the fear of a Jewish world conspiracy and elevated it to an almost mythic level. The work made its first appearance in 1895, an invention of the Russian czar's secret service, which modeled it on an earlier tract purporting to expose the machinations of the French emperor Napoleon III. The czar's forgers 'took this pamphlet, substituted world Jewry for the French emperor, and added a number of picturesque details borrowed from an obscure German novel,' writes Middle East scholar Bernard Lewis," Kenneth R. Timmerman, *Preachers of Hate: Islam and the War on America* (New York, NY: Crown Forum, 2003), 47-48.

Ottoman and thus joined the Ottoman army during WWI. When the Ottomans lost the war, he changed his allegiance to the Syrian cause, pressing for Arab autonomy and independence. He proved to be an aggressive outspoken nationalist, even making his presence known at the historic Syrian Arab Congress in 1920, where a coalition of leaders from Syria, Lebanon and Palestine declared independence for greater Syria. He was only in his early twenties.

That same year he was arrested and sentenced to ten years in prison for spear-heading anti-Jewish riots in Jerusalem, escaping justice by taking refuge in western Palestine.[56] Husseini single-handedly set the precedent for Arab-Muslim riots directed at Jews that continues to the present day in the region known as Palestine. British authorities granted him a surprise reprieve in 1921 and appointed him the position of Grand Mufti of Jerusalem at age 26, and one year later he was appointed the chairman of the Supreme Muslim Council, thus making him the most powerful Islamic leader, religiously and politically, in all of British Palestine. For the next fifty years he proved to be dictatorial and violent, directing his hostility primarily toward the Jews of Palestine, but secondarily toward the British and even fellow Arabs who threatened his hegemonic hold on power.[57] His animosity fueled major anti-Jewish riots in 1929 and 1936. By 1937 his antics deteriorated to sheer extremist terrorism and as a result was forced out of Palestine by the British. At this time he dedicated his passions to broadening his scope of Jewish hatred by seeking to partner with Mussolini and Hitler because of their anti-Jewish

---

56 "Husseini, Hajj," *Encyclopedia Judaica: Volume 8, He-Ir* (1971, 1973), 1133.
57 See Brog, *Israel's History*, 119, for details of his practice of murdering fellow Arabs in his circle who either had competing views or threatened his stranglehold on power among the Arabs of Palestine and beyond.

agendas. Husseini managed to secure a meeting with both dictators in late 1941, in the throes of WWII.[58] Husseini shared a common view with Mussolini, who said about the Jews: "They are our enemies…and there will be no place for them in Europe." He also echoed the message of the Nazis as is evident in this statement he made on a Berlin radio station in March of 1944: "Kill the Jews wherever you find them! This pleases God, history and religion."[59]

Husseini is known for introducing radical Islam to the modern world as well the practice of paying Arab terrorists for killing Jews and other infidels.[60]

After the Nazis lost the war Husseini fled Germany and escaped to various Arab strongholds until his death in 1974. Disillusioned by defeats in his collaborations with the Ottomans, then greater Syria, then the axis powers of WW II, and the Arab countries' loss to Israel in 1948, Husseini narrowed his focus of Arab independence to Palestine. Here he was successful, as he wielded an influence over the Palestinian Arab movement well into the 1960's. It was during the decades after 1948 when Arabs in former Syria began to identify themselves as "Palestinians" seeking a permanent national identity under the moniker of a yet-to-be established state called "Palestine." And according to Husseini, that could only happen with the complete subjugation of the Jews—a two state solution would never be an option.

Yasser Arafat picked up where Husseini left off in the pursuit of Arab independence in the land of Palestine to the

---

[58] Timmerman, *Preachers*, 107.

[59] Matthias Kuntzell, "National Socialism and Anti-Semitism in the Arab World," *Jewish Political Studies Review*, (2005), 17, 1-2.

[60] Brog, *Israel's History*, 123.

total exclusion of the Jews who lived there. Arafat is known as the greatest modern Arab Palestinian—but he was born in Cairo, Egypt, not Palestine. And in terms of ethnicity, he was an Arab, not a Palestinian. It was in Egypt where he became mesmerized by Husseini, a distant relative, who was in exile there. Arafat enrolled in Cairo university around 1950, which at that time was a hotbed for the Muslim Brotherhood, the Free officers and ardent Nazi sympathizers.[61] As a young man he became an assistant of the mufti's top deputy, allowing him extensive exposure and contact with Husseini, enabling him to be elevated to higher stature within the movement at an accelerated rate. Arafat quickly became the heir apparent. Early on he perfected acts of terror directed at the Jews. He also developed a knack for being coy and evasive about his true intentions in the support of anti-Semitism.

Arafat is best known for being associated with the Palestinian Liberation Organization (PLO), since its inception in 1963 under the sponsorship of the Arab League. Fronted as the platform for the eventual independent state of Palestine, the PLO actually was nothing more than a terrorist organization, with the goal of gaining independence "through armed struggle," with the goal of destroying Israel by "pushing them into the Great Sea."[62] Arafat was the chairman of the PLO from 1969-2004. By the 1970's the PLO was sponsoring at least eight different terrorist groups being monitored by Israel and the United States. Today the PLO/PA oversees more than ten terrorist groups including Hamas, Hezbollah, and Islamic Jihad, to name a few.

Arafat dedicated over fifty years of his life to committing acts of terrorism and later sponsoring acts of terrorism, all

---

61 Timmerman, *Preachers*, 113.
62Ibid., 204.

against the Jews with the goal of "liberating Palestine" from Israel, the "little Satan." One of his most notorious acts was committed on the world stage when on September 5, during the 1972 Olympics in Germany, a group affiliated with the PLO called the *Black September Organization* infiltrated Olympic Village in Munich, and slaughtered eleven members of the Israeli athletic team.

With his predecessor and hero, Husseini, Arafat was not shy about his utter disdain for the Jews as evidenced by a few of his public statements, almost always made in Arabic:

> "Whoever does not accept the fact that Jerusalem will be the capital of a Palestinian State, and only that State, can go drink from the Dead Sea and go to hell."[63]

> "Peace for us means the destruction of Israel....We shall not rest until the day when we...destroy Israel."[64]

> "We plan to eliminate the State of Israel and establish a Palestinian state. We will make life unbearable for Jews by psychological warfare and population explosion."[65]

In 2003, a popular secular American periodical summarized objectively Arafat's legacy to the world:

> Arafat...formed the al-Aqsa Martyrs Brigade because his experience has taught him that far from marginalizing him, terrorism pays. Let the record show: By November of 1974, Arafat's [PLO] had carried out the massacre of Israel's Olympic athletes, plane hijackings, letter bombs, the assassination of an American ambassador and Jordan's prime minister, the slaughter of 21 Israeli schoolchildren at Maalot, and the killing of 52 Israelis—mainly women and children—in Kiryat Shmona. Yet November 1974 was the month in which

---

63 *Arutz 7 News,* 6-26-00.
64 *El Mundo,* 2-11-80.
65 *Dagen,* 2-6-96.

he was invited to address the United Nations General Assembly, virtually unanimously.[66]

Despite the fact that Arafat's routine terrorist acts were public knowledge and went on for over fifty years, amazingly he was awarded the Noble Peace Prize in 1994! Ironically, Arafat never had any intentions of making peace with Israel. Until his death his stated position was that Israel had no rights in the land for he believed Israel had no rights to even exist. Arafat was the one responsible for propagating the popular nefarious notion (lie) among Arabs and Palestinian sympathizers that Israel never had a Temple in Jerusalem.

One of Arafat's greatest accomplishments, from an Arab Palestinian perspective, is that over the coarse of thirty-five years, he successfully created and pushed a false, historically-revised narrative that the whole world has embraced,[67] save a few countries, and that is that all of Palestine belongs to the Muslim Arabs, for it is their land by right, and Israel is an evil, occupying people that has no right to exist—a two state solution is not an option; and all acts of terrorism against the Jews of Palestine, including civilians is deserved.

Arafat did not live long enough to see one of his dreams come true, which was to have other countries recognize his fifty-year-old terrorist organization as a *bona fide* state. That happened in July 2019 when 138 out of 193 nations among the United Nations, recognized the PLO as the State of Palestine. As of August 2020, the United States does not

---

[66] *US News & World Report,* 9-29-2003.
[67] For example, Arafat was known to dogmatically assert that "a Jewish Temple never existed in the land of Palestine" along with other absurdities.

recognize them as an official state or nation. But give it time…that will change.[68]

Summary

Who are the Palestinians? We have now seen why this is such a difficult question. The prerequisites to unravel the dilemma require accurate understanding of the Bible, history and the nature of the modern conflict in the Middle East. One-dimensional, shallow answers don't suffice.

The word "Palestine" comes from the biblical word "Philistine." Technically, a Palestinian is a Philistine. The Philistines were not Arabs native to the land of Canaan. They were intruders to the land from the West and perennial enemies of God's people, Israel, and enemies of YHWH Himself. God predicted through His prophets that the Philistines would go extinct, and they did around the time of the Exile. As a result, there were no true ethnic Philistines in New Testament times nor are there any today.

Throughout history, Gentile nations have co-opted and even hijacked the word "Palestine," misappropriating it and applying it to the Promised Land that God gave to Abraham's descendants—the Jews. The Romans did it first in the 2nd century and the British followed suit in the 1920's after WWI. In the early 1900's, and for most of the past 2,000 years, Palestine referred to an area of land—it was a geographical designation—not an ethnicity, nationality or a people group. Prior to 1974, the people living in that land were known as

---

[68] In recent decades the UN has been overtly anti-Israel evidenced by their many hostile resolutions; frequently, Israel's only ally with the UN is the United States. "In November 2016, for instance, UN committees adopted ten different resolutions against Israel in a single day"; Craig Parshall, "The Legal Issues at the Nexus of the Conflict," *Israel, the Church and the Middle East*, 204.

Palestinian Jews and Palestinian Arabs. The Arabs in former Syria fine-tuned the obfuscation by personalizing, politicizing, and assimilating the name to their own ethnic and national identity, contrary to the clear teaching of the Bible, the public record of history, and all objective reality. As a result, confusion about who the Palestinians truly are will abound indefinitely and will further the irresolvable conflict between the Arabs and the Jews in the Middle East.

8

Hating the Jews

The Jews are a despised people. Today it's a popular thing to hate Israel. And that has been the case all throughout history. This chapter explores the reasons why that is the case from the Bible.

But first, consider a few modern-day examples that illustrate the case. The most popular anti-Semite[69] in America for the past fifty years has been Louis Farrakhan, leader of the Nation of Islam. In 2020 he delivered a public hate-filled 4th of July speech, riddled with slanderous comments about the Jews, calling them names such as "Satan" and "the enemy of God," and he encouraged his listeners to "fight Satan the arch deceiver [and] the imposter Jews who are worthy of the

---

[69] Historians make a distinction between "hating the Jews" versus being "anti-Semitic." Hating the Jews has been around for 4,000 years, since the enemies of Abraham, because of his unique religion and worship of the one true God, YHWH. Anti-Semitism is said to be of recent vintage, a by-product of 19th century race theory in Europe, where the Jews are despised because of their blood and DNA, (i.e., "racial superiority") not because of their religious practices; see Grayzel, 557-562. Gade summarizes it well: "The term anti-Semitism was coined by a German agitator, Wilhelm Marr, in 1879 to designate anti-Jewish campaigns then appearing throughout Europe. Since that time the term has been universally applied to any form of behavior, activity, or literature which evidences hostility toward the Jews"; Richard E. Gade, *A Historical Survey of Anti-Semitism* (Grand Rapids, MI: Baker Book House 1981), 7.

chastisement of God." This was on par for the long-time charismatic rabble-rouser, as he routinely calls Jews "bloodsuckers," "termites" and worse.[70]

If that wasn't divisive and despicable enough, he was cheered on and celebrated in the following by giants of pop culture including professional athletes (DeSean Jackson of the Philadelphia Eagles and former NBA players Stephen Jackson and Allen Iverson...and others), musicians (rappers 2 Chainz and Puff Daddy...among others), Hollywood "stars" (Nick Cannon, Stephanie Mills... and others), and a host of liberal Democrat politicians. For the first time in US history, we have anti-Semitic elected officials in power who are unabashed and unhinged anti-Semites. They voice their scathing biases routinely, using their public office as a platform. They spew with impunity.[71]

A couple more: Black Lives Matter, which has skyrocketed in popularity today, is a committed anti-Semitic, Marxist, anarchist organization, with a formal written manifesto that categorically condemns Israel and impugns all Jews.[72] The United Nations is blatantly anti-Semitic in bent and intent as evidenced by their flurry of biased anti-Israeli proposals and resolutions flooding out of New York in disproportionate waves for the past generation. I could give

---

[70] "Farrakhan Remains Most Popular Anti-Semite in America," *Anti-Defamation League*, July 15, 2020, adl.org; Gary Rosenblatt, "Is it Still Safe to be a Jew in America?," *The Atlantic*, March 15, 2020, theatlantic.com.

[71] The most notorious anti-Semites in office are Democrat congresswomen, Ilhan Omar from Minnesota and Rashida Tlaib from Michigan. Ayaan Hirsi Ali, "Can Ilhan Omar Overcome Her Prejudice?," *Wall Street Journal*, July 12, 2019, wsj.com; Beth Bailey, "Rashida Tlaib fails to apologize or correct her anti-Semitism," *The Washington Examiner*, January 28, 2020, washingtonexaminer.com.

[72] Yair Rosenberg, "From Left to Right, Jewish Groups Condemn 'Repellent' Black Lives Matter Claim of Israeli 'Genocide,'" *Tablet*, August 5, 2016, tabletmag.com.

countless more examples of the apparent rise in unrestrained anti-Semitism in American culture and around the world, but these suffice. Now onto the biblical background.

The Genesis of Jewish Hatred...the Canaanites

It is no surprise to the Bible that the world would be so thoroughly anti-Jewish. The Bible thoroughly explains why Jews are hated, by way of illustration and by way of prophecy. In many respects, the history of the Bible is a story of how the Jews have been despised by the world. And the derision from the world began with the ancestors of Israel, in the days of Shem, and it will extend to the end of world history, as clearly seen in the prophecies of Scripture.

Jewish hatred formally began with a prophecy God spoke through Noah around 2500 BC after Noah vacated the ark with his wife, Mrs. Noah, his three sons and their three wives. Noah planted a vineyard, and one day he drank too much and passed out naked in his tent. One of Noah's sons, Ham, saw his father's nakedness and mocked his father to his two brothers, Shem and Japheth. This was a blatant example of Ham dishonoring his father, which Moses would later decry as a sin worthy of death (Exod 20:12; 21:17). When Noah woke up, he realized what Ham had done to him and so pronounced a curse on him and his descendants, saying:

> Cursed be Canaan, a servant of servants, he shall be to his brothers (Gen 9:25).

Noah cursed Canaan directly and not Ham the actual perpetrator, signifying the curse was on Ham's entire lineage, for Ham was the father of the Canaanites (9:18; 10:15-19). The Canaanites eventually would prove to be archenemies of God's nation Israel. In addition to a generational curse on the

Canaanites, Noah also blessed the lineage of Shem:

> Blessed be the LORD, the God of Shem; and let
> Canaan be his servant (9:26).

Shem is the paradigm of later Israel and represents the lineage of God's election and blessing. From the loins of Shem came Abraham (Luke 3:34) and King David (Luke 3:31). Shem is the line that would bring Jesus the Messiah to Earth (Luke 3:23, 36).

The descendants of Ham, the Canaanites, would be servants of the Shemites. To be a "servant" was to be "subject to"—this speaks of inherent conflict. God promised the Canaanites would be perpetual enemies of the Jews. The Old Testament bears that out. Five hundred years after Noah, the Canaanites occupied all the land that God promised to Abraham (Gen 11:31). "Canaanite" came to be a general term referring to all the pagan people groups living in the land west of the Jordan.[73] The Canaanites were known for their

---

[73] "The term 'Canaan' has a complex history of use in and outside the Bible. It exhibits a fluidity in usage, varying between geographical locations and peoples. Its etymological history remains ambiguous as well. As a geographical reference it speaks generally of the strip of land that lies west of the Jordan River (modern Israel) and includes modern Lebanon and portions of Syria. By associating the name with Egypt, the table reflects an early period when the 'land of Canaan' was subject to Egyptian control....The boundaries of Canaan reported in [Genesis 10] v. 19 are especially significant for later Israel since it is the 'land of Cannan' that is the inheritance of Abraham (e.g., 15:18-21; 17:8). At times in the biblical record... 'Canaan' was used specifically of a people. At other places the term overlaps with many diverse peoples who inhabited Syro-Palestine. Canaan, for example, refers to the peoples who inhabiting the plains and the Jordan Valley (e.g., Num 13:29; Deut 1:7; Josh 11:3). And it may also specifically distinguish them from their immediate neighbors (e.g., 15:21; 34:30; Exod 3:17). On the other hand, 'Canaan' can refer to a variety of peoples living in proximity. This is the case of Esau's wives, who are said to be from the 'women of Canaan,' which include a Hittite, Hivite, and Ishmaelite (36:2-3). This fluidity is reflected by Ezekiel's commentary on

polytheism, lewd worship, divination, snake worship, sexual immorality, sacred prostitution, human sacrifice and other gross practices.[74] Sodom and Gomorrah were Canaanite cities illustrative of rampant Canaanite degradation (Gen 18-19). Abraham knew they were a dangerous and vile people and as a result did not want his son to marry a Canaanite woman (Gen 24:3). One thousand years after Noah's prophecy, Joshua would face the Canaanites in battles as he entered the Promised Land. God commanded Moses and Joshua to annihilate them from the land for they were a wicked people:

> [16]Only in the cities of these peoples that the Lord your God is giving you as an inheritance, you shall not leave alive anything that breathes. [17]But you shall utterly destroy them, the Hittite and the Amorite, the Canaanite and the Perizzite, the Hivite and the Jebusite, as the Lord your God has commanded you, [18]so that they may not teach you to do according to all their detestable things which they have done for their gods, so that you would sin against the Lord your God (Deut 20:16-18; cf. Lev 18:24-25).

After seven years of battle, Joshua led the Israelites into the land of Canaan to possess it. In the process, Joshua defeated thirty-one Canaanite kings (Josh 12). But Israel did not fully obey God and they allowed many Canaanites to remain in the land (Joshua 16:10). As a result, the Canaanites continued to be a menace to God's people for the next 900 years, even

---

Israel's beginnings, 'Your ancestry and birth were in the land of the Canaanites; your father was an Amorite and your mother was a Hittite' (16:3). Canaan as a people or location also commonly fluctuates with the term 'Amorites' (cf. e.g., 15:16; Josh 24:15-18; Judg 6:10; 1 Sam 7:14; Amos 2:10), though elsewhere 'Amorite' can be used of specific residents of Cisjordan's hill country and Transjordan kings Sihon and Og (e.g., Num 13:29; 21:21; Deut 3:8; Josh 10:5)....In later usage among the Greeks, 'Canaan' was used of Phoenicia"; Mathews, *Genesis 1-11*, 445-446.

[74] "Canaanites," *The Illustrated Bible Dictionary: Volume I*, Editor, J. D. Douglas (Wheaton, IL: Tyndale House, 1980), 235.

down to the time of Ezra when Jews compromised and engaged in the abominations of the Canaanites who still lived in their land (Ezra 9:1-2). Canaanites were so wicked the name "Canaanite" became a term of derision referring to that which is innately evil and opposed to God, so much so that God decreed "there will no longer be a Canaanite in the house of the LORD of hosts in" the future day of the Lord's reign on earth (Zech 14:21). All in all, the Canaanites proved to be treacherous enemies of the Jews for two thousand years!

The Egyptians-the Original Slave Owners

Another enemy of Israel from ages past is Egypt. The Bible mentions Egypt over 700 times, first occurring in Genesis 10:6 by the name Mizraim, which like Canaan, springs from the loins of Ham. Abraham had some encounters with the Egyptians. We noted one earlier: when his wife Sarah was taken from him by Pharaoh of Egypt (Gen 12:15). God struck the King of Egypt with a plague as a result. Abraham would later have a son with Hagar, Sarah's maid, who was an Egyptian (Gen 16:3). From Hagar and Abraham came Ishmael, whom God said would be a perpetual enemy to Israel.

Next, we meet the Egyptians in the days of Joseph, when he is sold by his brothers to the Midianites who take him to Egypt where he is purchased by Potiphar, an officer of Pharaoh (Gen 39:1). Here, around 1900 BC, the first Jew is a slave in Egypt. Previously, God warned Abraham that the entire nation of Israel would be enslaved and "afflicted" by Egypt for 400 years (Gen 15:13). Joseph eventually earned his freedom from the King of Egypt.

With the rise of a new king of Egypt, who knew not

Joseph, God's prophetic word to Abraham would come to fruition. The ruthless Pharaoh came to despise the Jews who were numerous and living as foreigners in his land—several hundred thousand strong by the time of Moses' birth. As a result, he subjected them to slavery and hard labor, appointing task masters over them (Exod 1:8-14). Threatened by their growing population, the Pharaoh gave an edict to the Hebrew mid-wives, insisting they kill all Hebrew male babies at birth. This was the first of several genocidal decrees issued against the Jews mentioned in the Bible.

When the Hebrew mid-wives failed to comply with Pharaoh's murderous order, he broadened it by commanding "all his people" to cast "every son" into the Nile River to be drowned (Exod 1:22). At three months old, Moses was cast into the Nile...inside of a floating basket and was rescued. When Moses became a man, Pharaoh intensified his persecution of the Jews by brutalizing them all the more through beatings (Exod 5:14) and depriving them of straw for their bricks while increasing the demand for production. In total, the Egyptians oppressed the Jews under the harsh yoke of slavery for 400 years! Then God moved with compassion, heard the prayers of His people, the children of Israel and said, "Now, behold, the cry of the sons of Israel has come to Me; furthermore, I have seen the oppression with which the Egyptians are oppressing them" (Exod 3:9).

God has reserved a special future judgment for the nation of Egypt for the way they abused God's people, the Jews. God declared to Moses, "Vengeance is Mine...He will avenge the blood of His servants and will render vengeance on His adversaries, and will atone for His land and His people" (Deut 32:35, 43). At the end of history, "in that day," God will strike Egypt like never before...eclipsing what He did with the Ten Plagues. "In that day, the Egyptians will become like women, and they will tremble and be in dread because of the waving of the hand of the LORD of hosts, which He is going to wave over them" (Isa 19:16). In fact, the entire chapter of Isaiah 19 is an oracle of judgment against Egypt that will be literally fulfilled with the coming of the Messiah. As with the Canaanites, there is future accountability coming from God himself toward the nations of old who treated Israel as an enemy instead of as a friend.

Ishmael, the Arabs and Islam

God promised to bless Abraham and give the land to his offspring, which began with a child of promise (Isaac) who would come through his legitimate wife, Sarah (Gen 18:9-10). But Abraham had an illegitimate son through Sarah's maid, Hagar. His name was Ishmael. Ishmael was Abraham's first-born, being about thirteen years older than Isaac. Their mothers, Sarah and Hagar, became enemies. In like manner, their two sons, Ishmael and Isaac, became enemies. And, as God predicted, their descendants (the Jews and the Arabs) became enemies...and remain enemies.

Abraham agreed to have relations with Hagar because Sarah had a lapse of faith in God's ability to provide a child through her in her old age (Gen 16:1-2). She was about 75 and had been waiting ten years since God promised an offspring. Abraham acquiesced to her lack of faith and so lapsed in his own faith. So he defiled his marriage by committing adultery. Nevertheless, God overrides all the sin with blessings, one of which was God's watch-care over Hagar and her son Ishmael (16:7-9).

Then the LORD made a unique promise to Hagar, saying "I will greatly multiply your descendants so that they will be too many to count" (Gen 16:10). In effect, God said Hagar's son, Ishmael, would be the father of a great nation of countless descendants. God reiterated this promise thirteen years later to Abraham saying, "And as for Ishmael, I have heard you: I will surely bless him; I will make him fruitful and will greatly increase his numbers. He will be the father of twelve rulers, and I will make him into a great nation. But My covenant I will establish with Isaac" (17:20-21).

So God would make Isaac a great nation and He would also make Ishmael a great nation. But they would be two very different kinds of nations. Through the nation of Isaac, the Jews of Israel, God would save the world through Jesus the Messiah. Through the nation of Ishmael, God would chasten the Israelites and many others. Listen to the rest of God's prophecy to Hagar at the time of Ishmael's birth:

> He [Ishmael] will be a wild donkey of a man,
> his hand will be against everyone,
> and everyone's hand will be against him;
> and he will live to the east of his brothers
> (Gen 16:12).

This verse reveals three key characteristics about the offspring of Ishmael. First, personally, in temperament, they will be "wild" and unrestrained. Second, socially, they will be warriors and fighters, being divisive and antagonistic—the opposite of peacemakers. And third, domestically, as to their domain, they will occupy the land "to the east" of Israel their "brothers." This is the land of the desert, the Middle East, which includes the vast lands of Arabia and beyond. And it is exactly what happened. Hagar gave birth to Ishmael, who in turn grew up, married and fathered many children, who in turn produced countless offspring, from which came the people of the East known as the Arabs.

The people of the East, the desert peoples, would be a perpetual thorn in the flesh to Israel. The sons of Ishmael would be the continual nemesis of the sons of Isaac. This prophecy was first literally fulfilled when Ishmael was just a teenager, about thirteen. Genesis 21:9 says that Ishmael was "mocking" Isaac, the Jew, at the time of his weaning when Isaac was just a baby. As a result, the antagonistic Ishmael was banished to "the wilderness" (21:14), but with the promise of God, who again told Hagar, "I will make a great nation of him" (21:18). From there Ishmael grew strong, became a man "and he lived in the wilderness and became an archer" (21:20). Being described as an "archer" emphasizes he would be a warrior typified by strife and warfare. Genesis 25:18 says Ishmael "settled in defiance of all his relatives."

Genesis 25:12-18 delineates the areas in the East that the Ishmaelites occupied, populated and dominated as represented by their twelve tribal heads: Nebaioth, Kedar, Adbeel, Mibsam, Mishma, Dumah, Massa, Hadad, Tema, Jetur, Naphish and Kedemah. These became the Arabs of the desert in the east who lived in defiance of Israel. A noted commentator highlights the implications:

Havilah and Shur therefore formed the south-eastern and south-western boundaries of the territories of the Ishmaelites, from which they extended their nomadic excursions towards the north-east as far as the districts under Assyrian rule, i.e. to the lands of the Euphrates, traversing the whole of the desert of Arabia, or dwelling from the Euphrates to the Red Sea. Thus, according to the announcement of the angel, Ishmael "encamped in the presence of all his brethren.[75]

---

75 C. F. Keil and F. Delitzsch, *Commentary on the Old Testament: The Pentateuch* (Peabody, Massachusetts: Hendrickson Publishers, 1989), 265; Fruchtenbaum notes these 12 names are the "twelve Arab nations or

Ishmael lived around 1900 BC. That was 3,900 years ago. Amazingly, Ishmaelite Arabs have perpetually inhabited the deserts of the Middle East, including Arabia, since that time. And since the seventh century AD, Arabia and much of the Middle East has converted *en masse* to Islam. Today, the nations surrounding Israel are predominantly Arab and Muslim and live in defiance toward Israel, just as God said they would. Arabs and Muslims are not synonymous, but in the seventh century AD Islam found fertile soil in the Arab culture to blossom, grow and flourish as a new-found religion in Arab lands. Commenting on the twelve Arab tribes listed in Genesis 25, one scholar makes the obvious historical connection between Arabs and Islam:

From these tribes sprang the Arab peoples who have contributed much, perhaps more than most, to the world's culture and the world's cruelty. The atrocious African slave trade was largely the work of the Arabs. The abysmal spiritual darkness of Islam is yet another Arab contribution to the woes of the world. And persistently, to this day, Israel's

---

tribes" God promised in 17:20; Arnold G. Fruchtenbaum, *Ariel's Bible Commentary: The Book of Genesis* (San Antonio, TX: Ariel Ministries, 2009), 395. Another commentary says, "this genealogy of Ishmael establishes the connection between Ishmael and his twelve sons with the Arabs of later biblical and postbiblical history...evidence for associating Ishmael with the Arabs is that Ishmael's second oldest son Kedar is identified with 'Arabia' in Is 21:13-17 and Ezk 27:21. Other evidence to associate Ishmael with the Arab peoples is historical, with 'Geshem the Arab' of Neh 6:1 being possibly mentioned in a fifth-century BC inscription as "king of Kedar," linking the Arabs with the second eldest son of Ishmael. Also Arabs, since the rise of Islam in the seventh century (2,700 years after Abraham) have maintained their descent from Ishmael, and Jewish and Christian tradition has generally accepted this," *The Moody Bible Commentary*, ed. Michael Rydelnik and Michael Vanlaningham (Chicago, IL: Moody Publishers, 2014), 84.

bitterest foes have been of Ishmaelite stock.[76]

Today there are 22 Arab nations that surround Israel, a federation called The Arab League. These 22 Arab nations are all Islamic, with the average percentage for each state being at 90% or more Muslim. Most of these nations are totalitarian Islamic theocracies that employ Sharia law and do not tolerate other religions, and virtually all of them consider Israel a sworn enemy. They all hate the Jews.

This sad reality is in keeping with what God said about Ishmael almost 4,000 years ago—"he would be a wild donkey of a man." Defiance was in his blood, and it hasn't changed since. God said there would never be peace between Ishmael and the Jews. They will be at each other's throats perpetually, until Christ's Second Coming, and that remains true to this very day. No world leader or American President is going to be able to mediate the establishment of a legitimate long-term peace treaty between the Jews and Arabs, especially Islamic Arabs. The only peace will be silence during rearmament in the midst of war. That is what God's Word says.

Esau, the Edomites and Herod

In addition to the Canaanites, Egyptians, and Ishmaelites (Arabs), another people group known as the Edomites—descending from Esau and his progeny—despised Israel and the Jews from the time of their origin. The story begins in Genesis 25. Isaac was married to Rebekah, who was barren, so she prayed to the LORD and He opened her womb. She became pregnant with twins. Immediately the boys in her womb "struggled together," a harbinger of the extensive

---

76 John Phillips, *Exploring Genesis: An Expository Commentary* (Grand Rapids, MI: Kregel Publications, 1980), 201.

struggles yet to come. God gave a prophecy about her twins while in the womb:

> Two nations are in your womb;
> and two peoples will be separated from your body;
> and one people shall be stronger than the other;
> and the older shall serve the younger
> (Gen 25:23).

The first-born twin was Esau, also known as Edom (Gen 25:30). The younger twin was Jacob, the child of promise in the line of the coming Messiah. In this prophecy God predicted these two men would war with each other and their descendants would as well. God blessed Jacob the younger son and elected him to be the progenitor of the twelve tribes of Israel. God changed Jacob's name to Israel as a sign of the divine blessing. Esau despised his brother Jacob all his days because Jacob was blessed by God (27:41).

Like Cain, whose heart became poisoned from jealousy-driven hatred toward his brother, so also Esau nurtured a grudge in his soul toward Jacob to the point that he purposed in his heart the following sentiment: "I will kill my brother Jacob" (vs. 41). The descendants of Esau, the Edomites, purposed in their hearts to do the same—to kill the Israelites at every chance. For centuries they pursued this cause.

Esau came to despise God as well. Esau eventually settled in the mountains south of the Dead Sea and the region became known as Edom, "Idumea" in Greek (see Ezek 36:5 in the KJV). Numbers tells of how the Edomites denied their brother, Jacob, the Israelites, through their land during the time of the Exodus (Num 20:17). Moses sent messengers ahead asking, "Please let us pass." Edom's response was cruel and heartless: "You shall not pass through us, or I will come out with the sword against you" (20:18).

Edom would fight against Israel and their kings for the next 700 years. God would in hindsight pronounce a curse on Esau for his wicked and carnal ways, first around 850 BC through the prophet Obadiah and then formally in a simple dirge written by Malachi around 450 AD:

The oracle of the word of the LORD to Israel through Malachi. "I have loved you," says the LORD. But you say, "How have you loved us?" "Was not Esau Jacob's brother?" declares the LORD. "Yet I have loved Jacob; but I have hated Esau, and I have made his mountains a desolation and appointed his inheritance for the jackals of the wilderness" (Mal 1:1-3).

Edom's hatred toward the Jews reached a crescendo when they became known as the Idumeans with the spread of the Greek Empire after the fourth century BC.

Herod the Great, an Idumean, became king of Judea under Rome in 37 BC. In a sense, the enmity between Esau and Jacob was continued in Herod's attempt to murder Jesus. The Idumeans participated in the rebellion of Jerusalem against Rome and were defeated along with the Jews by Titus in A.D. 70. Ironically, the Edomites applauded the destruction of Jerusalem in 586 B.C. (cf. Ps 137:7) but died trying to defend it in A.D. 70. After that time they never were heard of again. As Obadiah predicted, they would be "cut off forever" (v. 10); and "no survivor shall remain of the house of Esau" (v. 18).[77]

Why the World Hates the Jews

From the foregoing it is clear that the Jews are a despised people. And the Bible predicted this would be the case and it showed through history how it was the case. Since their

---

[77] *The MacArthur Study Bible* (1997, 2017), 1288-89.

inception 4,000 years ago Israel has been hated by the Canaanites, the Egyptians, the Philistines,[78] the Ishmaelites and the Edomites. The last 2,000 years of world history show they have been hated by even more nations all over the world—by Rome, Spain, Russia, Germany, 57 Islamic countries, and more. Today, they are just as despised.

The big question is *Why?* Why have the Jews been hated all throughout history, since their very existence all the way up until the present day? Once again, the Bible has a clear answer and it is manifold—there are several reasons and they are all inter-related. Let's consider them now.

God Loves Israel
The Bible is clear that God loves Israel. God said to Israel, "I have loved you...I have loved Jacob" (Mal 1:2). And His love for Israel is an everlasting, eternal love. God told Jeremiah that as long as the sun, moon and stars remain in place, so also will Israel be God's people (Jer 31:35-37). Israel is God's elect (Isa 45:4), YHWH's bride (Hosea 1-14), God's eternal possession (Ezek 16:8), His everlasting covenant people (Gen 17:7), and very offspring and Son (Isa 63:8). And God's love and eternal commitment to Israel is not contingent upon Israel's worthiness or desirability, but upon God's sheer sovereign grace and divine, gratuitous love (Deut 7:7-8).

Whatever God loves, the world hates. Because God has loved Israel from her origin, Israel would be hated by the world. Israel's enemies were God's enemies. God said it this way to Moses: "I will be an enemy to your enemies and an adversary to your adversaries" (Exod 23:22). Or consider this Psalm:

[1]O God, do not remain quiet;

---

[78] See previous chapter on Palestine.

Do not be silent and, O God, do not be still.
²For behold, Your enemies make an uproar,
And those who hate You have exalted themselves. ³They make
shrewd plans against Your people,
And conspire together against Your treasured ones.
⁴They have said, "Come, and let us wipe them out as a nation,
That the name of Israel be remembered no more"
(Ps 83:1-4).

This Psalm makes clear that God's "enemies" hate His people "Israel" so much they will try to obliterate Israel from the face of the earth. The world hates God and all He stands for. The Bible says, "do you not know that friendship with the world is hostility toward God? Therefore whoever wishes to be a friend of the world makes himself an enemy of God" (James 4:4). The "world" here is the fallen, cursed evil system, including humans and demons, that opposes God. This definition of the world is more defined by the Apostle John:

> Do not love the world nor the things in the world. If anyone loves the world, the love of the Father is not in him. For all that is in the world, the lust of the flesh and the lust of the eyes and the boastful pride of life, is not from the Father, but is from the world. The world is passing away, and *also* its lusts; but the one who does the will of God lives forever (1 John 2:15-17).

Those in the world hate God because they love their sin and despise His holiness and the accountability they have before Him as Creator and Judge (John 3:19-20). The world's hatred for God and things of God is the deepest and strongest kind of hatred there is. As such, the unbelieving world is wicked to the core and hates Israel and the Jews instinctively because of the historic relationship God has had with them as His special, covenant people. And because God's love for Israel extends into the future, eternally, the world will always hate

Israel and the Jews with an unmitigated passion. The re-
curring utopian dream of eradicating racial prejudice in the
world is delusional, especially when it comes to hating the
Jews. Racism, like poverty, is with us until Christ comes in
glory.

Jesus was a Jew

The world hates the Jews because Jesus was a Jew (an
Israelite from the tribe of Judah) and the world hates Jesus.
Jesus said, "The world...hates Me" (John 7:7). This is a
universal, timeless, transcendent truism. There are no
exceptions. All unbelievers hate Christ in their very souls.
Some are very good at covering it up. But Jesus' divine,
omniscient diagnosis stands. Unbelievers hate everything
about Jesus, especially His narrow teachings (which is in the
Bible), His people (true believers), His Church, His holiness,
His warnings of judgment and calls to repentance, and God
His Father. The world most hates the fact that Jesus is the
Judge of every soul (John 5:22) and upon death they will have
to bow the knee to Him (Phil 2:10) while every one of their
deeds, thoughts and motives from life will be exposed and
accounted for (Rev 6:15-17). Psalm 2 is concise, yet a graphic
prophetic description of the world's hatred reaching its zenith
toward Jesus the Messiah.

Satan Hates the Jews

Satan was originally created as a good angel by God. He fell
into sin by his own selfish will and was then cursed by God.
Since his fall he has reigned as the supreme demon in the
invisible spiritual realm, the heavenlies (Eph 6:12). He is
utterly, incorrigibly corrupt. There is no good in him. He
hates God with every molecule of his being. And he hates
everything associated with God. Because Israel is God's elect

nation, Satan hates them with a venomous fury.

The Bible says Satan is "the god of this [fallen, corrupt] world" (2 Cor 4:4). John says, "the whole world lies in the power of the evil one" (1 John 5:19). Satan is "the prince of the power of the air, of the spirit that is now working in the sons of disobedience" (Eph 2:2). He is the tireless, perennial enemy of God's people who "prowls around like a roaring lion seeking someone to devour" (1 Pet 5:8). He is the deceiver, the slanderer, the destroyer and the non-stop accuser of the brethren (Rev 12:10).

Chapters 1 and 2 of Job expose Satan's tactics. He is working behind the scenes, within God's limitations, with the goal of mocking God and destroying God's plan and people. Satan has been working from the beginning to undermine God's plan of salvation that would come through the promise given to the progenitors of Israel, culminating in the greatest Jew, Jesus the Messiah. Satan tried to poison the Messianic line countless times in the Old Testament; he inspired Pharaoh and Herod in an attempt to slaughter all Hebrew males; he empowered Haman's attempt to wipe out the Jewish race completely (Esther); and in the coming Great Tribulation (Matt 24:21) Satan will once more seek to annihilate the Jews completely (Rev 12:1-17).

Jesus said Satan was a murderer from the very beginning (John 8:44). Hatred and murder are his nature. The past two thousand years gives much evidence of Satan's hatred of the Jews evidenced by the relentless and unprecedented world-wide assault on the Jews as a people and Israel as a nation from all quarters.[79]

---

79 Hitler's concentrated hatred and persecution of the Jews can only be explained in light of a greater spiritual reality—Hitler and his people were

Bad Theology In the Church

Unbelievers, the world and Satan aren't the only ones who have hated the Jews through the ages. Two thousand years of Church history reveals professing believers have at times fared not much better than unbelievers in anti-Jewish sentiment and actions. Martin Luther is not the only culprit here. Constantine made it a crime to convert to Judaism. The preacher Ambrose of Milan celebrated the burning of a synagogue. Chrysostom, the "golden-mouther" preacher, called the Jews "devils," "wild beasts" and said, "I hate the Jews for they have the law and they insult it." In the 1200's Aquinas supported the edict of the Catholic Church's Fourth Lateran Council (1215) when Pope Innocent III decreed that Jews were required to wear a distinguishing yellow badge in front and back. The Muslims had done this to the Jews years before.

The Badge was to be a mark of shame to drive the Jews out of European society.[80] This ghastly discriminatory practice would be resurrected by Hitler in 1941 Nazi Germany. The Roman Catholic Crusades (1096-1271), the Medieval Papal inquisitions and the Roman Catholic Spanish Inquisition (1478) are additional infamous examples of the Jews getting caught up in the middle of the corrupt and capricious wrath of the "Church's" systematic attempts to purge all defectors. Horrific examples abound. All these and more are documented by Barry Horner in *Future Israel: Why Christian Anti-Judaism Must Be Cancelled.*[81] Barry accurately shows how Christians throughout the centuries have

---

driven by Satan himself in their attempt to slaughter all Jews. Scripture is clear on that (Eph 2:2). See Erwin Lutzer's, *Hitler's Cross*, which makes this plain (Chicago, IL: Moody Publishers, 1995).

[80] Grayzel, *A History*, 312.

[81] Horner, *Future Israel* (Nashville: B & H Academic, n.d.).

disparaging views of Israel and the Jews due to bad theology, or more specifically compromised hermeneutics—allegorical hermeneutics adopted from the days before Augustine, popularized by Augustine and ratcheted up by various Christians up to the modern day. The common denominator in it all is the false notion that the Church has displaced Israel and so now the Church is the new "spiritual" Israel. That is bad theology.

God Chastens His Children

God is in total control; He's completely sovereign (Ps 115:3). Nothing happens apart from His knowledge, permission, will or purpose. And since the history of the world is riddled with anti-Semitism, wars against Israel, and hatred toward the Jews, it only follows that God has something to do with it. And He does!

God said, "Those whom I love, I reprove and discipline" (Rev 3:19). Elsewhere God reminds His people:

> you have forgotten the exhortation which is addressed to you as sons, "My son, do not regard lightly the discipline of the Lord, Nor faint when you are reproved by Him; For those whom the Lord loves He disciplines, And He scourges every son whom He receives." It is for discipline that you endure; God deals with you as with sons; for what son is there whom *his* father does not discipline? But if you are without discipline, of which all have become partakers, then you are illegitimate children and not sons. Furthermore, we had earthly fathers to discipline us, and we respected them; shall we not much rather be subject to the Father of spirits, and live? For they disciplined us for a short time as seemed best to them, but He *disciplines us* for *our* good, so that we may share His holiness. All discipline for the moment seems not to be joyful, but sorrowful; yet to those who have been trained by it, afterwards it yields the peaceful fruit of righteousness (Heb 12:5-11).

As long as His people are sinful, God will always need to discipline or chasten them. This was true of God's Old Testament covenant people as well as New Testament saints. God said, "Israel is My son" (Exod 4:22) and "I am a father to Israel" (Jer 31:9). As God's covenant children, Israel would always be subject to God's refining process of loving parental discipline. From the very beginning God warned Abraham that His people Israel would be subject to persecution. Before Isaac was born God said, "Know for certain that your descendants will be strangers in a land that is not theirs, where they will be enslaved and oppressed four hundred years" (Gen 15:13). For four centuries the Egyptians brutalized and oppressed the Jews. Why did that happen? One main reason is simply because God said it would.

After Moses led nearly two million Israelites out of Egypt, while they were in the wilderness before entering the Promised Land, God gave Moses new revelation, much of which he wrote down and comprises our current Pentateuch. In Leviticus 26 God spoke to Moses and the Jews in the context of the covenant, specifying various blessing for obedience and curses for disobedience. If they obeyed, God would bless them with good weather, bounty in the land, safety from all enemies, fertility among the people and His presence would abide with them (vv. 3-13). The Old Testament records that Israel's times of blessing due to their consistent obedience was scant from 1400-430 BC.

If they disobeyed, God promised He would chasten them with disease, stolen crops, defeat to surrounding enemies, bad weather, famine, plague, pestilence, cannibalism, and worst of all, they would be displaced from the land by foreign enemies and would be scattered among the nations of the world...where they would always remain the minority (Lev

26:14-39). Israel's disobedience was regular century after century, and true to His Word, God brought these specific consequences time and time again.

God goes on to make it clear to Moses that He will bring these curses upon Israel for the purpose of discipline, to woo His covenant people back to Him, so that under the pressure of suffering and persecution they would "confess their iniquity" (vs. 40) and be "humbled" (vs. 41). When that desired result comes about then God promised He would restore His people because of His commitment to the covenant He made with Abraham, Isaac and Jacob, the fathers of the Jews (vs. 42). The apex of that restoration would be bringing them back to "the land" (vs. 42).

A few years later, in the land of Moab, just before Moses' death, the great prophet reminds the Jews of what God said years earlier in Leviticus 26, this time going into even greater detail about the chastening they would receive if they disobey God (Deut 28:15-68).[82] Again, the culmination and apex of God's discipline for Israel would be their displacement from the Promised Land by enemies from without:

> Moreover, the LORD will scatter you among all peoples, from one end of the earth to the other end of the earth...Among those nations you shall find no rest; and there will be no resting place for the sole of your foot; but there the LORD will give you a trembling heart, failing eyes, and despair of soul. So your life shall hang in doubt before you; and you will be in dread night and day, and shall have no assurance of your life (Deut 28:64-66).

---

82 For an excellent explanation of future implications of the Abrahamic and Mosaic Covenants toward the nation of Israel, see William Barrick, "Intercovenantal truth and Relevance: Leviticus 26 and the Biblical Covenants," *MSJ* 21/1 (Spring 2010): 81-102.

Israel failed time and again and as a result the above dismal prospect became reality for them. The Old Testament bears this out. One could argue that this paragraph of doom is a good description of the Jews' existence the past 2,000 years as they have been scattered all throughout the world, as a persecuted, despised minority people wherever they find themselves. Note, this isn't just "bad luck" for the Jews. Verse 64 says the LORD is the one who causes this desolation. And He does it for a purpose. His purpose is to purify Israel in holiness and to bring about ultimate restoration for them as a nation before Him. The chastening God brings upon Israel is efficacious and will bring the desired result: repentance and obedience (Deut 30:2), and "then the LORD your God will restore you from captivity, and have compassion on you, and will gather you again from all the peoples where the LORD your God has scattered you" (vs. 3). Historically, God displaced Israel for their disobedience first in 722 BC when Assyria invaded northern Israel, then again in 586 when Babylon invaded Judah. In each instance Jews were scattered among the nations away from their homeland. Waves of Israelites have incrementally trickled back to their homeland, but never in a wholescale manner.

The height of Israel's disobedience is when they rejected their own Messiah, Jesus of Nazareth. Jesus came as the Savior of the world and as the King of Israel in fulfillment of specific numerous Old Testament prophecies (John 12:16). "He came to His own, and those who were His own did not receive Him" (John 1:11). Only a small minority of Israelites accepted Him as their Messiah; the majority, including the Jewish leadership, rejected Him and called for His execution. Jesus categorically denounced the Jewish leaders for their hypocrisy and unbelief (Matt 23). He wept over Jerusalem for their wholesale rejection of His Messiahship (vs. 37). The sin of that generation of Jews, Jesus said, would "not be forgiven, either in this age or in the age to come" (Matt 12:32). The Gospel of John portrays "the Jews" as the quintessential enemies of Jesus and His ministry. Near 80 times John uses the phrase "the Jews" as a synonym for the Pharisees, the Scribes and the Sadducees, who are overtly in opposition to Christ's teaching and work (cf. John 1:19; 5:10; 8:48; 18:12; 19:7).

After blessing the Jews for three-plus years with faithful preaching of the good news, healing all the sick and performing countless miracles that blessed the masses, He was rewarded with betrayal and condemnation. He came as the Son of the Father, the very incarnation of YHWH—and to reject Jesus was to reject God Himself. And that is what the Jewish nation did—they willfully, with hardened hearts, turned their back on God and His King.

The Jewish religious leaders spear-headed a staged trial based on trumped up charges, accusing the sinless Savior of blasphemy, which warranted the death penalty. They successfully got an audience with the Roman governor, Pilate, who concluded after an inquiry: "I find no fault in him" (John 19:4). But the Jewish leadership managed to manipulate the Jewish crowds who gradually amassed around the fraudulent trial, coaxing them to scream for Jesus' blood. And they complied, shouting in unison and in rage, "Crucify him! Crucify him!" (Matt 27:20-23; John 19:9). The Jewish people demanded the death of their own innocent Messiah, who was sent as a gift from heaven.

Pilate washed his hands in front of the Jewish mob and declared, "I am innocent of this Man's blood; see to that yourselves" (Matt 27:24). Their collective response is chilling. Scripture says, "all the people said, 'His blood shall be on us and our children'" (vs. 25). At that critical juncture in history, an entire generation of Jews invoked a corporate curse on all their descendants by demanding the blood of the Messiah. Many would say that their curse on themselves came to fruition as evidenced by 2,000 years of being stigmatized by many as "Christ-killers." Countless enemies of the Jews through the centuries have used the fact that Jesus was rejected by the Jews as justification for persecuting the Jews, from the Roman Catholic Church, to Islamic regimes, to secular governments, to crazed totalitarian dictators, to fringe political movements, to even, occasionally, respected, but misguided, individuals like Martin Luther.

So the Jewish nation was culpable for the death of the Messiah. But at the same time, the death of Jesus—the timing, the purpose and the mode—was all according to the plan of God as determined by Him from eternity past (Isa 53; Ps 22; Acts 2:23). There was a remnant of Jews who believed when Jesus came 2,000 ago,[83] but there was also a national rejection, and God is holding Israel as a nation accountable for that rejection. Israel as a nation is currently hardened toward Jesus, and as such cannot be in right relationship with the Father. Paul tells us that hardening is only partial and temporary, and in the future, Israel as a nation will repent and be saved. In the meantime, God will continue to discipline

---

[83] Don't forget the obvious—Jesus and the 12 Apostles were Jews; the Church born on Pentecost with the 120 saints plus the 3,000 baptized the first day were all Jewish. Paul was a Jew. The entire church for the first five years of its existence was strictly Jewish. "Though the number of the sons of Israel be like the sand of the sea, it is the remnant that will be saved" (Isa 10:22; cf. Jer 23:3; Zech 8:12; Rom 9:27). God made it clear long ago that that there would always be a faithful remnant within the nation of Israel.

and chasten Israel, even subjecting them to persecution and suffering until they soften. Until that future day the Jews will continue to be a despised people the world over.

Summary

The Jews are a despised people the world over. This is actually proof that the Bible is true because from the very beginning God warned Abraham and Israel that they would be hated. That enmity began with the Canaanites around 2000 BC. The Hebrews were slaves in Egypt for centuries. The Philistines harassed the Jews all throughout Old Testament history. The Ishmaelites and the Arabian desert peoples have hated the Jews since the days of Abraham up until 2020. The Edomites and the Idumeans tried to annihilate the Jews. And Scripture gives several reasons for this hatred: God loves Israel; Satan and the world hate God and all that is His; Jesus was a Jew and the world hates Jesus. Christians through the ages who adopted a compromised hermeneutic often fell into wrong, harmful views about Israel. And also, God allowed Israel to be subjected to hatred and persecution as a form of loving discipline and chastening. This chastening will eventuate in Israel's corporate and national repentance in the future, at the end of the age.

9

The Future of Israel

What is the destiny of the nation of Israel? Is there still a future on earth for Israel in God's program? Is Israel still God's elect nation? These are highly contested questions among Christians today and have been historically throughout the Church age. Scholarly books and articles continue to be published on these complicated and volatile questions—too many to read and assess. There are actually several views on the topic among Evangelicals, but the main ones can be put into three basic views or categories.

First, there are those who believe God is punishing the Jews and will continue to punish them until the end of the age for their unpardonable sin of rejecting Jesus, their own Messiah. Albertus Pieters (1897-1987), former Bible professor of Western Seminary in Holland, Michigan, Loraine Boettner (1901-1990), Princeton grad and popular Bible teacher and author and Stephen Sizer (b. 1953), former Anglican priest in England are three modern examples of people who have written vindictively against the Jews and Israel from a "Christian" perspective. Fortunately, this view seems to be a minority view, albeit an influential one. Sadly at times in history this view was the majority view in the Church and proved to be very destructive and dishonoring to Christ and the gospel.[84]

Second, there are those who say Israel is no different than any other nation on earth today. God is not dealing with nations anymore; there are no theocracies as there were in the Old Testament. God is dealing with individuals, not nations, through gospel proclamation. An unsaved Jew today is no different than an unbelieving agnostic, atheist or cultist—they all need the simple gospel of Jesus. Christians who hold this view typically say all the promises made to Israel in the Old Testament are fulfilled by the Church. In other words, the Church is the new spiritual Israel. Historically, John Calvin at times seemed to have this view. Today, many popular Bible teachers in the US hold this view, including Alistair Begg and many others.

And finally, there is the third view, which states that Israel is still God's special nation. However, they are temporarily in a state of rebellion, but will repent in the future. That is the view I will defend from Scripture in this chapter.

A Proper Foundation

Before delving into the main arguments to defend view three, it is important to be aware of prerequisite presuppositions that drive this debate on Israel's standing before God now and in the future. To have a meaningful discussion beyond the superficial one we need to consider a proper hermeneutical approach, a biblical ecclesiology and a wholistic eschatology.

To have a biblical perspective on Israel it is required of the

---

84 The reader is referred to three recent books that expose this blight on the church while giving the proper biblical view on how the church should view Israel and the Jews: *Forsaking Israel* by Larry Pettegrew, *et al.,* and two books by Barry E. Horner, *Future Israel* and *Eternal Israel.*

Bible interpreter to maintain a consistent hermeneutic, and particularly the grammatical-historical approach to interpreting the Bible. The alternative is to resort to various forms of allegorically-driven approaches to interpretation, which inevitably default into inconsistent, subjective and overly-symbolic interpretations of various passages, especially when trying to make sense of God's countless promises to Israel that He made to them in the Old Testament.[85] A proper ecclesiology will ensure that an illegitimate supersessionism (replacement theology) doesn't creep in, whereby all the promises that God made to Israel become somehow swallowed up and subsumed by the Church, which is deconstructed and then reconstructed as the entity identified as the "new spiritual Israel," an identification found nowhere in the New Testament. A wholistic, exegetical eschatology will ensure that the whole council of God is taken into consideration when making as assessment about Israel's present and future status before God. Too often eschatologies on Israel are selective, or truncated, neglecting key passages in Scripture that speak directly and fully to the topic at hand.[86]

---

[85] "In the history of the church the eschatological or prophetic portions of Scripture have suffered more from inadequate interpretation than any other major theological subject. The reason for this is that the church turned aside from a normal and grammatical literal interpretation of prophecy to one that is nonliteral and subject to caprice of the interpreter. This false approach to interpreting prophecy is contradicted beyond question by the fact that so many hundreds of prophecies have already been literally fulfilled." John F. Walvoord, *Every Prophecy of the Bible* (Colorado Springs, CO: Chariot Victor Publishing, 1999), 9.

[86] This is where the unique contribution to systematic theology by Arnold Fruchtenbaum is much appreciated; the expanded version of his 466-page PhD dissertation from New York University called, *Israelology: The Missing Link in Systematic Theology* is a welcomed and authoritative source for this discussion.

Seven Considerations

There are many arguments to be made in defense of the idea that God still cares about Israel as a nation and that He has a special future plan for them, but I will consolidate them to seven main ones.

God's Promise to Israel was an Everlasting Promise

The first of which has already been addressed thoroughly in this book, namely God's promise to Abraham to make him a nation, was an eternal promise that would last "forever." And the endless nature of this promise was based on the foundation of God's character, His unconditional election and the oath He swore unto himself to see it through. He told Abraham that His covenant with Abraham's descendants, the Jews, was an "everlasting covenant" and that He would give Israel "the land of Canaan for an everlasting possession" (Gen 17:7-8).

God Promised to Gather all Israel Back into the Land at the End of the Age

From the beginning of their origin God promised Israel they would be spread around the world as a means of chastening but at the end of the age He would bring them back to the land once for all. This national ingathering is yet future. Israel has a future in God's program. Consider these Old Testament promises:

> then the Lord your God will restore you from captivity, and have compassion on you, and will gather you again from all the peoples where the Lord your God has scattered you. If your outcasts are at the ends of the earth, from there the Lord your God will gather you, and from there He will bring you back. The Lord your God will bring you into the land which your

fathers possessed, and you shall possess it; and He will prosper you and multiply you more than your fathers (Deut 30:3-5).

And He will lift up a standard for the nations and assemble the banished ones of Israel, and will gather the dispersed of Judah from the four corners of the earth (Isa 11:12).

"For behold, days are coming," declares the Lord, "when I will restore the fortunes of My people Israel and Judah." The Lord says, "I will also bring them back to the land that I gave to their forefathers and they shall possess it" (Jer 30:3).

Say to them, "Thus says the Lord God, 'Behold, I will take the sons of Israel from among the nations where they have gone, and I will gather them from every side and bring them into their own land; and I will make them one nation in the land, on the mountains of Israel; and one king will be king for all of them; and they will no longer be two nations and no longer be divided into two kingdoms'" (Ezek 37:21-22).

"Also I will restore the captivity of My people Israel, and they will rebuild the ruined cities and live *in them*; they will also plant vineyards and drink their wine, and make gardens and eat their fruit. I will also plant them on their land, and they will not again be rooted out from their land which I have given them," says the Lord your God (Amos 9:14-15).

"Behold, I am going to deal at that time with all your oppressors, I will save the lame and gather the outcast, and I will turn their shame into praise and renown in all the earth. At that time I will bring you in, even at the time when I gather you together; indeed, I will give you renown and praise among all the peoples of the earth, when I restore your fortunes before your eyes," says the Lord (Zeph 3:19-20).

Thus says the Lord of hosts, "Behold, I am going to save My people from the land of the east and from the land of the west; and I will bring them *back* and they will live in the midst of

Jerusalem; and they shall be My people, and I will be their God in truth and righteousness" (Zech 8:7-8).[87]

God's Unconditional Covenants were Made with Israel, Not the Church
God made three covenants that began to find their fulfillment with Christ's first coming and will be completely fulfilled at His Second Coming and reign on the earth. Those covenants include the Abrahamic, the Davidic and the New. The Abrahamic Covenant promised a coming seed who would bless all the families of the earth (Gen 12:1-3). Jesus the Messiah was that seed. The Davidic Covenant promised that the coming Messiah would be a descendant of David and would inherit an eternal throne and an eternal kingdom (2 Sam 7:11-17; 1 Chron 17:10-15). The New Covenant promised national restoration and forgiveness for Israel, complete and eternal forgiveness, the indwelling Spirit, and more (Jer 31:31-34; Isa 59:21; 61:8-9; Ezek 34:25-27; 36:25-27; 37:26-28).

These three covenants were made with Israel in the Old Testament. They were not made with Gentiles or the Church. Gentiles partake in some of the blessings of these covenants, but their complete fulfillment awaits the national restoration of Israel at the end of the age.[88] All three covenants are complementary and overlap. Technically, the David and New

---

[87] Hat tip to *The MacArthur Study Bible*, 1256, for the compilation.
[88] For example, the Davidic Covenant has not yet been fulfilled. Jesus is not sitting on a literal throne ruling over earth in Jerusalem. He is sitting in heaven at the right hand of the Father. Jesus has the authority to rule from David's throne, and at the end of the age He will assume that position....literally....on the earth; for a thorough exposition of this topic see Michael J. Vlach, *He Will Reign Forever: A Biblical Theology of the Kingdom of God* (Silverton, OR: Lampion Press), 569-579.

Covenants flow from the Abrahamic Covenant.[89] These unilateral, unconditional, eternal covenants that God made with the nation of Israel remain intact. Paul said plainly, that to the "Israelites...belongs...the covenants...and the promises" (Rom 9:4) and that His "gifts and the calling" to Israel are "irrevocable" (11:29).

God Made Numerous Promises to Israel that have Yet to be Fulfilled
Some estimates say the Bible gives over 1,000 prophesies and about half of those have been fulfilled already, meaning nearly 500 more await fulfillment in the future.[90] The first 500-plus were literally fulfilled. The next 500 will be literally fulfilled. It is estimated that of the 500 already fulfilled, 109 were prophecies about Jesus specifically, fulfilled with His first coming.[91] 321 more will be fulfilled with His second coming. Most of these 1,000 prophecies were made to Israel, by an Israelite prophet regarding events related somehow to Israel. Of the remaining hundreds of prophecies yet to be fulfilled, many of them pertain specifically to Israel.

The many remaining unfulfilled prophecies God made to Israel and about Israel must be understood literally. It is not right to say, as many Christians do, that the remaining prophecies yet to be fulfilled that were originally promised to Israel will now be fulfilled by the Gentile Church instead. Or worse is to say they will not be fulfilled literally but rather are fulfilled "spiritually"...whatever that means. To do so is playing fast and loose with hermeneutics. Also, when we say

---

[89] See, "The Davidic Covenant," by Michael A. Grisanti for the continuity of the covenants, *TMSJ* 10/2 (Fall 1999): 233-250 and "The New Covenant" by Larry D. Pettegrew: 251-270.
[90] Walvoord, *Every Prophecy of the Bible*, 7.
[91] Tim LaHaye, *The End Times Controversy*, "Introduction," ed. Tim LaHaye and Thomas Ice (Eugene, OR: Harvest House Publishers, 2003), 15.

promises that God made to Israel in the future that have not happened yet will never happen literally is to make God a liar. When God promised Israel the land forever, He meant forever. When He called the nation Israel His "elect," He meant elect forever.

We could examine dozens and dozens of prophecies that God made to Israel in the Old Testament that have not been fulfilled yet, but that would take up too much space. So we will showcase one that illustrates the point, making it obvious that there are prophecies that God made to Israel that have not yet been fulfilled that literally still must happen in the future. And if that is true, then it becomes obvious that the nation of Israel still has a special role in God's future plan for human history and beyond.

Take Zechariah 12-14 as exhibit A. Zechariah 12-14 is known as "the little apocalypse" since it corresponds to end-time events described in the book of Revelation, the big apocalypse. Zechariah was a post-exilic priest who wrote this prophecy around 480 BC. In chapters 12-14 Zechariah prophesied that God would protect Jerusalem when "all the nations of the earth" come against her for war (12:3). The Lord Himself will go to war against all the nations to defend Jerusalem when His feet "stand on the Mount of Olives" (14:4). The Lord standing on the Mount of Olives is an obvious reference to Jesus returning in the future to Jerusalem at the end of the age. The war described in detail in these chapters has been properly called the Battle of Armageddon. A host of Bible interpreters from all persuasions agree Zechariah 12-14 seems to parallel the events described in Matthew 24-25 and the Book of Revelation. Where they disagree is on the "when" the events happen that are described in these chapters.

Christian preterists say all the events already took place back in 70 AD. Amillennialists say the events depicted apply to the Church, which is the new "spiritual Jerusalem," and it does not apply to the real, literal historic Jerusalem. This, then, is not a promise to Jews but to Gentile Christians. They also say the events happened already, such as during the Maccabean period,[92] or the events described are not in reference to a specific event but rather are general truisms that happen all the time to believers[93] ...an idealist interpretation. To take a preterist, amil or idealist view is to categorically ignore the plain meaning of the three chapters. God is talking to the nation of Israel about specific events that will happen at the end of the age that culminate at Jesus' Second Coming to the Mount of Olives.[94] It is not only crazy, shallow dispensationalists who take a literal, and therefore, futurist view of Zechariah 12-14, for none other than the highly respected Reformed theologian James Montgomery Boice made the case for a literal view, despite his amil theology.[95]

The fact is, Zechariah opens this end-times prophecy saying, "the word of the LORD concerning Israel" (12:1). Ironically, Calvin's comment on this verse says this passage is about "the church." But this prophecy is about Israel, not the Church. Zechariah 12-14 refers to "Israel," "Jerusalem," "the

---

[92] Matthew Henry's suggestion.

[93] i.e., Calvin and many others.

[94] For a helpful, plain exegetical interpretation based on the Hebrew text of all three chapters, using a grammatical-historical hermeneutic, see Arnold Fruchtenbaum, "The Little Apocalypse of Zechariah," *End Times Controversy*, 251-281.

[95] "Nothing in this chapter fits historical events. So either the chapter is descriptive of events yet future, or it is to be considered figuratively as describing this present age...This will not do [taking it figuratively]"; James Montgomery Boice, *The Major Prophets* (Grand Rapids, MI: Kregel Publications, 1986), 221.

inhabitants of Jerusalem," "the clans of Judah," "the house of David," "the Mount of Olives," "Uzziah king of Judah," "Benjamin's Gate," "Rimon south of Jerusalem," and more references and allusions to ethnic Israel. Zechariah establishes the timing of these events by saying they will transpire "in that day," a specific eschatological reference to the end of the age. He uses that phrase 17 times in these three chapters. Jesus' feet will stand on the Mount of Olives "in that day" (14:4).

The reader is encouraged to read and study Zechariah 12-14 at face value, in context, using a consistent legitimate hermeneutic, and one can only conclude by saying, "These events described have never happened in history and must be yet future." And they are. In addition to Zechariah 12-14, many prophetic passages about Israel's future can be added to the list, some of the most prominent ones include Psalm 2, Isaiah 27, Isaiah 60-66, Jeremiah 30-33, Ezekiel 36-7, Ezekiel 38-39,[96] Ezekiel 40-48, Daniel 12:1-3, Joel 2-3, and Amos 9:11-15. From these passages it is clear that Israel has a specific place in God's future program.

Jesus said Israel had a Future
Jesus clearly believed and taught that Israel had a long-term

---

[96] The popular 18th century English Presbyterian commentator, Matthew Henry, said we are not to look for the literal meaning in Ezekiel 38-39 but instead the symbolic one; with that approach he concludes Ezekiel 38-39 is not a future one but a past one, in the days of Antiochus; dispensationalists and futurist interpreters on the other hand correctly see Ezekiel 38-39 as literal events that transpire in Israel at the end of the age, either prior to the seven year Tribulation (the view of Randall Price, *The Coming Last Days Temple* [Eugene, OR: Harvest House Publishers, 1999], 454), during the Tribulation (the view of Charles Dyer, *The Bible Knowledge Commentary: Old Testament*, "Ezekiel," 1300) or at the end of the 1,000 year Millennium (the view of Ralph H. Alexander, *The Expositor's Bible Commentary: Volume 6*, "Ezekiel," ed. Frank E. Gaebelein [Grand Rapids, MI: Zondervan, 1986], 932).

future in God's kingdom program.

He spoke about five specific events in their future that all relate to each other. He predicted they would reject Him, that the Romans would attack Jerusalem, that there would be a historical period of desolation where Israel would be dominated by Gentiles, that there would be a future Tribulation centered in Israel and finally that there would be a restoration of Israel as a nation in a future kingdom on earth.

First, Jesus predicted that Israel would reject Him as their Messiah and there would be long-term ramifications for doing so. Just days before His death Jesus made this pronouncement about Israel:

> Jerusalem, Jerusalem, who kills the prophets and stones those who are sent to her! How often I wanted to gather your children together, the way a hen gathers her chicks under her wings, and you were unwilling. Behold, your house is being left to you desolate! For I say to you, from now on you will not see Me until you say, "Blessed is He who comes in the name of the Lord!" (Matt 23:37-39).

Jesus' statement contains a curse and a blessing for Israel. The curse is that as a nation, God will leave Israel "desolate" for rejecting their Messiah. From the time of Christ's crucifixion God was temporarily abandoning Israel as His special people. But Jesus also gives hope here. He says Israel will be desolate "until" a future day when they see Jesus and embrace Him as Messiah. Jesus did not say "unless" Israel repents, but "until." In other words, their repentance is guaranteed by God. That day is coming and will be fulfilled just as numerous Old Testament prophets predicted. In the future, on a corporate scale, the nation of Israel will turn to Christ and say, "Blessed is He who comes in the name of the Lord!"

Second, during His final week on earth Jesus predicted the Romans would attack and destroy Israel's capital, Jerusalem.

> For the days will come upon you when your enemies will throw up a barricade against you, and surround you and hem you in on every side, and they will level you to the ground and your children within you, and they will not leave in you one stone upon another, because you did not recognize the time of your visitation (Luke 19:43-44).

Four decades after this prediction it was fulfilled in every last detail. In 70 AD the Roman general, Titus, set a barricade up against Jerusalem, surrounded the city for a prolonged period starving the inhabitants, leveled it to the ground, including the temple. This event was the formal catalyst of the "desolation" spoken of by Jesus against Israel noted in Matthew 23.

Third, in addition to the immediate judgment that would come upon unbelieving Israel as depicted in Luke 19, Jesus spoke of judgment upon Israel at the end of the age as well, at the time of the Great Tribulation. Jesus describes the coming worldwide tribulation in Matthew 24:4-31. It is clearly still a future event because the tribulation climaxes when Jesus returns to earth (vs. 30). The tribulation will be an unprecedented universal event for Jesus says, "there will be a great tribulation, such as has not occurred since the beginning of the world until now, nor ever will" (vs. 21). And Jesus says Israel is the epicenter of the coming world-wide tribulation as He warns that those who will live in "Judea" should flee to the mountains (vs. 16). Jesus also says the tribulation will end with His glorious physical return to earth (vv. 29-31). When He returns He will judge His enemies and establish His kingdom on earth and usher in the Millennium.[97]

Fourth, Jesus said that Israel would be abandoned by God for a time, but again, only a temporary time. He said, "Jerusalem will be trampled under foot by the Gentiles until the times of the Gentiles are fulfilled" (Luke 21:24). Again, the word "until" is key—Gentile domination over Israel will end. Jesus said a fulfillment of that time period is coming—it will end—and then God will resume His relationship with Israel, His special nation.

Fifth, Jesus promised His twelve Jewish apostles, who were a part of the theocracy of Israel, that they would rule with Him on the earth, in the Promised Land, in the future kingdom, just as all the Old Testament prophets predicted (Dan 7:27; 9:26-27). Jesus promised His Jewish apostles the following:

> And Jesus said to them, "Truly I say to you, that you who have followed Me, in the regeneration when the Son of Man will sit on His glorious throne, you also shall sit upon twelve thrones, judging the twelve tribes of Israel" (Matt 19:28).

On a separate occasion Jesus repeated this great reality to His apostles:

> You are those who have stood by Me in My trials; and just as My Father has granted Me a kingdom, I grant you that you may eat and drink at My table in My kingdom, and you will sit on thrones judging the twelve tribes of Israel (Luke 22:28-30).

The "regeneration" refers to the future new age when God

---

[97] It is important to remember that the idea of a real, literal Tribulation at the end of the age was not some crazy idea invented by John Nelson Darby in the 1800's or by sensationalist theologians at Dallas Seminary in the early 1900s. God told Moses around 1400 BC that "in the latter days" (i.e., the end of human history), there will be a "tribulation" that Israel must live through (Deut 4:30-31; cf. Dan 12:1; Rev 3:10).

renovates the fallen world, which the Old Testament prophets described as a future age of glory (Isa 66); the period John the apostle said was 1,000 years, and which Jesus described as "the Kingdom." This is when Jesus will be "restoring the kingdom to Israel" (Acts 1:6). Jesus refers to Himself as "the Son of Man," a title taken from Daniel 7 that describes Israel's Messiah. Jesus said He will sit on a throne, and that throne will be in Jerusalem. The twelve Jewish apostles will rule with Him, in Jerusalem, over the twelve tribes of Israel. Clearly Jesus taught and believed that Israel still had a future in God's program.

A summary of Jesus' view of Israel's future based on His teaching can be outlined from the preceding statements just highlighted. Jesus said that Israel would be judged by God for rejecting Him as the Messiah. That judgment would be severe, but temporary and it formally began with the Romans sacking Jerusalem in 70 AD. The divine chastening would continue throughout history, two-thousand years so far, a period defined by Jesus as "the times of the Gentiles." It will culminate in the future coming world-wide Great Tribulation. At the end of the Tribulation, Jesus will return in glory and restore Israel as a nation in their land and Jesus will rule from His throne in Jerusalem. His faithful twelve Jewish apostles will also rule with Him in glory in Jerusalem over the nation of Israel for 1,000 years in fulfillment of countless Old Testament prophecies.

Paul Taught that Israel has a Future

The most comprehensive and systematic teaching in the New Testament on the fate of the nation of Israel is given by Paul in Romans chapters 9 through 11. In Romans 8 Paul argues that no one can be separated from the love of God. This assertion begs the question: "If that is true, then how come Israel has been separated from God?" Paul answers that questions in chapters 9, 10 and 11.

Paul wrote Romans around AD 56 toward the close of his third missionary journey. By AD 56 it was clear that the majority of Israel had rejected Jesus and the Christian gospel—only a few Jews believed. Under Paul's leadership, the gospel was exploding among the Gentiles. Twenty-five years after Christ's death it seemed to many that Israel had been separated from God. How could this be?

Paul answers the question directly in these chapters by highlighting his main points when he says in effect, "Yes, it appears that the nation as a whole has rejected Christ, but their rejection is only partial, providential, and temporary." Paul reminds his readers that not all Jews have rejected Christ. Many believed. For the first five years of the Church it was totally Jewish. All the founding apostles were Israelites. The majority of the nation did not believe, but the faithful few among Israel did embrace Jesus as Messiah. Paul argues this point by quoting Isaiah: "Though the number of the sons of Israel be like the sand of the sea, it is the remnant that will be saved" (Rom 9:27; cf. 11:4-5; Isa 10:22). As such, the apparent rejection on the part of Israel is not total, but partial. Paul says emphatically, "a partial hardening has happened to Israel" (Rom 11:25). So technically, no one can legitimately accuse all Jews of rejecting Christ and being Christ killers, as has been heard by anti-Semites through the centuries. Nor could anyone accuse God of not keeping His original promise given in the Abrahamic Covenant when He said Israel was His possession forever.

In addition to Israel's rejection of the Messiah being partial, their unbelief was also providential. God's providence refers to his beneficial work and the directing of human events through secondary causes, like the choices of humans, even bad choices. Paul argues in Romans 11 that through Israel's sinful choice of rejecting Jesus, God created a channel for allowing Gentiles to believe. God sovereignly turned Israel's national disobedience into blessing for gentiles all over the world. Paul says, "their rejection is the reconciliation of the world" (vs. 15). God has grafted Gentiles into the vine of blessing to woo the nation of Israel to faith in their Messiah by way of divine jealousy: "by their transgression salvation has come to the Gentiles, to make them [Israel] jealous" (vs. 11). This wooing will work, for in the future Israel will be won over to the Messiah on a national level. Paul asserts Israel "will be grafted in, for God is able to graft them in again" (vs. 23).

Israel's unbelief currently is partial, providential and also temporary. Israel as a nation will not go on in unbelief forever. Paul says the whole nation, as an entity, will repent in the future at the end of the age.

> For I do not want you, brethren, to be uninformed of this mystery—so that you will not be wise in your own estimation—that a partial hardening has happened to Israel until the fullness of the Gentiles has come in; and so all Israel will be saved; just as it is written, "The Deliverer will come from Zion, He will remove ungodliness from Jacob. This is My covenant with them, when I take away their sins" (Rom 11:25-27; cf. Isa 59:20).

Paul declares unequivocally that "all Israel will be saved" (Rom 11:26). In context, this corporate event is clearly future—Israel as a nation will turn to the Messiah, and it will happen when "the fullness of the Gentiles has come in" (Rom 11:25). This is exactly what the Old Testament taught.

Zechariah said in the last days just prior to the final coming of the Messiah in glory, God

> will pour out on the house of David and on the inhabitants of Jerusalem, the Spirit of grace and of supplication, so that they will look on Me whom they have pierced; and they will mourn for Him, as one mourns for an only son, and they will weep bitterly over Him like the bitter weeping over a firstborn (Zech 12:10).[98]

Paul goes on to warn Gentiles Christians about having a condescending attitude toward Israel and the Jews for their national unbelief: "do not be arrogant toward the branches [Israel]; but if you are arrogant, remember that it is not you who supports the root [Israel], but the root supports you" (Rom 11:18). Sadly, many Gentiles Christians through the ages have arrogantly looked down their noses in judgment of Israel as though they have no future in God's program. Nothing could be further from the truth. A day is coming when all Israel shall be saved!

Revelation Teaches Israel has a Future

The book of Revelation tells how the biblical drama and God's sovereign plan for sinners through the ages ends. Revelation has some challenges, but it is not impossible to understand. Actually, it's pretty clear. After all, Evangelicals

---

[98] Many think that only shallow dispensationalists take Romans 11:26 literally. But that is not the case. Interpreting Romans 11:26 at face value is a common view among many respected Reformed theologians. Geerhardus Vos understands Romans 11 to be talking about a future ethnic Israel, "the receiving back of the unbelieving majority of the Jews into favor...[a national conversion] on the largest of scales at the predetermined point in the future"; *The Pauline Eschatology* (Phillipsburg, NJ: Presbyterian and Reformed, Rep 1991 [1930]), 87-88; see also Vos, *Biblical Theology* (Carlisle, PA: Banner of Truth, 2000), 79: "Israel in its *racial* capacity will again in the future be visited by the saving grace of God [Rom. 11.2, 12, 25]."

claim to believe in "perspicuity"—the clarity of Scripture. That doctrine applies to Revelation just as much as it does to Philippians and the Gospel of John. Revelation 6-22 explains how the world ends. It is all future still, for the most part. And it has much to say about Israel. And the bulk of what it says can be found in the Old Testament prophecies as well as in the teachings of Jesus and Paul. And in the future, the nation of Israel figures prominently.

Revelation 6-18 describes in detail the future Great Tribulation (Rev 7:14). This is the same tribulation described by Daniel, the prophet of Israel (7:23-27; 9:27), who said it would last seven years. Jeremiah, another prophet of Israel, called it "the time of Jacob's trouble" (30:7). The future tribulation is designed to chasten Israel and bring her to repentance. John does not mention the Church at all in Revelation 6-18, a good indication that the seven-year chastening period is not intended for the Body of Christ, but rather for recalcitrant Israel.

There are three main references to Israel in Revelation. The first is where John describes 144,000 men "from every tribe of the sons of Israel" (7:4). He then lists the tribes by name, beginning with Judah and ending with Benjamin (7:8). These 144,000 are real individuals who will live during the tribulation. They are the famed coming "Jewish evangelists." These Jewish believers will be "sealed" with supernatural protection by God so they can fulfill their special charge of responsibility of witnessing for Christ during the world's most troublesome hour. John refers to the 144,000 again in 12:17 calling them the "seed" of the woman: Israel. Here they are portrayed as victorious witnesses in the last half of the seven-year tribulation, in an ongoing battle against Satan and his anti-Christ. John mentions the 144,000 again in 14:1-4, where they are pictured with Christ on Mount Zion, in Israel at the beginning of the Millennium where they reign in glory:

> Then I looked, and behold, the Lamb *was* standing on Mount Zion, and with Him one hundred and forty-four thousand, having His name and the name of His Father written on their foreheads. ²And I heard a voice from heaven, like the sound of many waters and like the sound of loud thunder, and the voice which I heard *was* like *the sound* of harpists playing on their harps. ³....no one could learn the song except the one hundred and forty-four thousand who had been purchased from the earth. ⁴These are the ones who have not been defiled with women, for they have kept themselves chaste. These *are* the ones who follow the Lamb wherever He goes. These have been purchased from among men as first fruits to God and to the Lamb.

A second main reference to Israel is in Revelation 12:1-17, where Israel is described as a "woman" and Satan is called "the dragon." This chapter is a succinct overview of the history of Israel's battle with Satan that culminates in the Great Tribulation. In the future tribulation Satan will persecute the nation of Israel, seeking to destroy her, but in the end, Israel will be rescued by God in the "wilderness."

Consider a third reference to Israel in Revelation 21:

> And he carried me away in the Spirit to a great and high mountain, and showed me the holy city, Jerusalem, coming down out of heaven from God, having the glory of God. Her brilliance was like a very costly stone, as a stone of crystal-clear jasper. It had a great and high wall, with twelve gates, and at the gates twelve angels; and names *were* written on them, which are *the names* of the twelve tribes of the sons of Israel (10-12).

Here John mentions the nation of Israel in the new heaven and the new earth, after the tribulation and after the 1000-year reign of Christ. Believing Israel will be showcased by

God for all in heaven to see forever by way of a visual reminder in the twelve gates of the heavenly city. This is God's reminder for all time that Israel, His special called nation, is never to be forgotten by anyone. Christians would do well to remember Israel now and not wait until then.

These three passages from John's Revelation clearly show that Israel has a distinct future in God's salvation program.

Summary

Does the nation of Israel have a special place in God's future program? From the examination of many Bible passages in this chapter, the answer is an emphatic, "Yes!" There are disparate views by Christians on this question. But the diversity of conflicting views does not preclude a clear, definitive biblical answer. Key to answering the question are the prerequisites of a proper hermeneutic and examining the whole council of God. Utilizing a proper hermeneutic will prevent the illegitimate approaches to Scripture that result in replacement theology and allegorization.

This chapter argued that ethnic Israel has a distinct role to play in the future in light of seven biblical arguments. This is an important point because history shows that when Christians fail to recognize the special place national Israel has in God's future program, anti-Jewish sentiments tend to seep in, many times in subtle "harmless ways" that later give way to unbridled hostility.[99] To guard against this trend, we looked at seven truths from Scripture. First, God's promise to

---

[99] This happened over a twenty-year period in Luther's life. Oberman notes, "The basis of Luther's anti-Judaism was the conviction that ever since Christ's appearance on earth, the Jews have had no more future as Jews"; Heiko A. Oberman, *The Roots of Anti-Semitism In the Age of Renaissance and Reformation*, translated from the German by James I. Porter (Philadelphia: Fortress Press, 1981), 46.

Abraham about God's commitment to Israel was an "everlasting" promise, based on God's vow with Himself. There is no expiration date. Second, God promised many times that He would ultimately restore Israel back to their land of promise at the end of the age. Third, God made His unconditional covenants with Israel, and those covenants are still in play. Fourth, hundreds of promises that God made to Israel remain unfulfilled. God will fulfill them all, literally, in the future. Zechariah 12-14 is a compilation of such promises. Fifth, Jesus taught that Israel had a future. He promised He would rule over Israel on earth during His kingdom reign, with twelve Jewish apostles ruling by His side (Matt 19:28). Sixth, Paul taught that Israel had a future. Right now, the nation of Israel is partially and temporarily hardened, being chastened by God, but will repent and be restored at the end of the age (Rom 9-11). Seventh, the Book of Revelation teaches that Israel has a future as described in chapters 6-19, which depict real, future, literal events. God will use 144,000 ethnic Israelites to represent Him during the coming Great Tribulation and the whole nation will be restored by Christ. A redeemed nation of Israel will mourn over the One Whom they have pieced and cry out, "Blessed is He who comes in the name of the Lord."

10

The Christian Attitude Toward Israel

What is the proper Christian attitude toward Israel and the Jews? Sometimes that is not clear even among believers. But it should be, because the Bible is clear on the matter. The better question is, "What is the biblical perspective today about Israel as a nation and Jews individually?" People who call themselves Christians have diverse views on every topic; the Bible on the other hand does not change with time, cater to the whims of man, nor contradict itself. Its views on any given topic are clear, true, authoritative, transcendent, divine and inspired by God (2 Tim 3:16). And the Bible has much to say about the believer's attitude toward Israel. Let's consider several.

Don't be Spiritually Arrogant and Dismissive

The first thing for Christians to consider is to not be spiritually arrogant over Israel's widespread unbelief and rejection of Jesus as Messiah. If you have not already, or recently, read Romans chapters 9 through 11 in one sitting where Paul addresses this very issue, then do it now. He wrote those three chapters to caution Gentile believers against any kind of bias, partiality or air of ethnic superiority they might feel as they look down in condescension on Israel and the Jews. Paul's argument is simple. He points out that Israel was God's original people of favor; through Israel God brought the gospel and the Savior to the world; God also gave the covenants to Israel, and those covenants will be ultimately fulfilled by Israel, forever. Israel is the original root of God's blessing; saved Gentiles are branches who were saved by being attached to that original root. Don't become spiritually arrogant by judging the Jews, otherwise you run the risk of getting cut off from the root as a form of God's judgment. Consider Paul's warning here:

> [18]do not be arrogant toward the branches; but if you are arrogant, *remember that* it is not you who supports the root, but the root *supports* you. [19]You will say then, "Branches were broken off so that I might be grafted in." [20]Quite right, they were broken off for their unbelief, but you stand by your faith. Do not be conceited, but fear; [21]for if God did not spare the natural branches, He will not spare you, either (Rom 11:18-21).

God knew Christians would be tempted to be spiritually proud and, as a result, treat unbelievers, particularly Jewish unbelievers, with contempt. Remember that in Romans 11 Paul is warning Gentile Christians not to be arrogant toward unbelieving Jews. Two thousand years of Church history shows that too many Gentile Christian leaders have been arrogant and condescending toward unbelieving Jews.[100] Some prominent Christian leaders through the centuries that have had arrogant views toward Israel include Justin (100-

---

[100] For a helpful discussion of how anti-Jewish sentiments began to formally trickle into wide acceptance into the Church through the writings and teachings of the early Gentile church fathers, see Larry Pettegrew, "The Curious Case of the Church Fathers and Israel," in *Forsaking Israel*, 33-34.

165),[101] Irenaeus (130-202), and Origen (184-253), whose statements against Israel were quite insidious, such as the following,

> They [the Jews] will never be restored to their former condition. For they committed a crime of the most unhallowed kind, in conspiring against the Savior...It accordingly behoved that city where Jesus underwent these sufferings to perish utterly, and the Jewish nation to be overthrown, and the invitation to happiness offered them by God to pass to others—the Christians.[102]

He grossly distorts the truth by laying all the blame for Christ's death at the feet of the Jews and at the same time ignores the fact that many Jews believed. The New Testament does not blame the Jews alone for Christ's death. The Bible also blames Pilate the Roman (John 19:16), Herod the Idumean (Luke 23:8-12), the Roman soldiers who crucified Him (John 19:2-3; Acts 2:23), the whole world of sinners throughout history whose sin put Him on the cross (including yours and mine) (Luke 22:19) , and most of all, Satan (Rev 12:1-4), God's greatest enemy. Blaming only the Jews for Jesus' death is an egregious and stilted prostitution of the truth. And as was pointed out in an earlier chapter, there were plenty of Jews who believed in Christ, including the apostles, the 120 saints, the 3,000 converted on Pentecost and all those in the church for its first five years of existence—it was an entirely Jewish Christian church.

John Chrysostom (347-407), Archbishop of Constan-

---

[101] "The word 'Israel' is applied to the Christian Church for the first time by Justin Martyr c. A.D. 160. It is a symptom of the developing take-over by Christians of the prerogatives and privileges of Jews"; Peter Richardson, *Israel In the Apostolic Church* (New York: Cambridge University Press, 1969, 2005), 1.

[102] Origen, "Against Celsus" (Whitefish, MT: Kessinger, 2013), 4:22.

tinople, took spiritual conceit against the Jews to new heights with his infamous, hate-filled haranguing Homilies against the Jews. Here's one sound-bite:

> They [the Jews] became dogs, and we became the children....Although such beasts are unfit for work, they are fit for killing. And this is what happened to the Jews: while they were making themselves unfit for work, they grew fit for the slaughter....the synagogue is not only a brothel and a theater; it also is a den of robbers and a lodging for wild beasts....the Jews say that they, too, adore God. God forbid that I say that. No Jew adores God![103]

Ambrose of Milan (340-397), Jerome (347-420), and Augustine (354-430) also held unfavorable views of Israel and the Jews. Augustine's influence here ran deep and wide throughout Church history. The most notorious Jewish bigot in popular culture was probably Martin Luther (1483-1546). The German Reformer had moderate views of unbelieving Jews early in his life but toward the end he lost his bearings. Three years before his death he wrote a 65,000-word tract called "On the Jews and Their Lies." By way of comparison, the book you are holding now is about 45,000 words. Here's just a few lines from Luther's literary tirade:

> The blind Jews are truly stupid...Now just behold these miserable, blind, and senseless people...their blindness and arrogance are as solid as an iron mountain...be on your guard against the Jews, knowing that wherever they have their synagogues, nothing is found but a den of devils...Moreover, they are nothing but thieves and robbers...they lie so clumsily and ineptly that anyone who is just a little observant can easily detect it... eject them forever from this country...away with them!...we all can be rid of the unbearable, devilish burden of the Jews...Nor dare we make ourselves partners in their

---

103 John Chrysostom, "Against the Jews," Homily 1: Tertullian.org.

> devilish ranting and raving by shielding and protecting them,
> by giving them food, drink, and shelter...First to set fire to
> their synagogues or schools and to bury and cover with dirt
> whatever will not burn, so that no man will ever again see a
> stone or cinder of them.

There is no defending Luther's scathing, hateful words directed at Jewish unbelievers. It's completely contrary to the New Testament ethic, the gospel, and the mission of the Church (Rom 12:14; 17-21). Hey Christian—do not think more highly of yourself than you ought (Rom 12:3). And when it comes to unbelieving Israel, don't be arrogant.

Be Compassionate like Jesus

Jesus saved His harshest words for the religious Jewish leadership who rejected Him (John 8). But when it came to the masses and crowds of average Jews who did not believe, he was often patient, compassionate, prayerful, broken-hearted and forgiving toward them. Jesus dealt with sinners on an individual basis. He did not lump all people together. When condemnation was warranted against unbelieving Jews, He delivered (Matt 23). When grace was required, He was the model. The Gospels tell of the encounter Jesus had with a rich young ruler. The man was a Jewish, legalistic, spiritually proud leader of the synagogue. The man approached Jesus, knelt before the Savior and asked, "What must I do to inherit eternal life?" (Mark 10:17; cf. Matt 19:20; Luke 18:18). The man did not do what Jesus asked and ended up leaving unredeemed because of his spiritual pride and blindness. Jesus did not denounce him. Instead, the Bible says, "Jesus felt a love for him."

Jesus was compassionate over the lost city of Jerusalem, for He wept over it at the end of His life as He desired to see the many lost Jewish souls get saved. The quintessential act of compassion was when, on the cross, Jesus asked the Father to forgive (Luke 23:34) the very crowd of Jews who cried for His blood before Pilate as they screamed, "Crucify Him!" (Matt 27:20-23).

Remember that Israel still has a Future with God

God's promise to Abraham in Genesis 12 still stands: God will bless those who bless Israel and God will judge those who curse Israel. Paul makes this clear in Romans 11. He states plainly that "all Israel shall be saved" and that Gentile Christians should not be conceited toward Israel. Today there is no theocracy as there was in the Old Testament, so God does relate to the nation of Israel differently for now. The Church, the Body of Christ, is whom God is betrothed to. Nevertheless, it is in one's best interest not to formalize a position of antagonism, hostility or bias against God's Old Testament Bride, Israel.

A couple common questions I get about the phrase in Romans 11:26 where Paul declares, "all Israel will be saved," is "Does this mean that every Jew in the future will be saved?" and another, "Does this mean all Jews are presently being saved?" The answer to both questions is "No." Context narrows the answer as do Old Testament prophecies that speak directly to promises of a national repentance of Israel. The context of Romans 11 is talking about how God will redeem Israel in the future, at the end of the age; it is not talking about all Jews getting saved during the church age. Furthermore, Paul the former Jewish Rabbi was being specific about the future salvation of national Israel in light of many Old Testament prophecies. He quotes extensively from the Old Testament in Romans 11 to establish his arguments, including 1 Kings, Deuteronomy, Isaiah, Psalms, Jeremiah and Job. He alludes to even more, like Genesis, 2 Kings, 1 and 2 Samuel and more. The Book of Revelation actually shows how God will save Israel in the future. God will use the Great Tribulation to chasten, purge, purify and woo unbelieving Israel, bringing them to the point of redemption by the end of the Tribulation. Zechariah 12:8-9 says that in total two-thirds of the Jews will be "cut off" or purged through the process and God will save the remaining one-third of them…every single one. This purging process is further described in detail in Ezekiel 20:33-38 and Zechariah 12:12-14. So to answer the question, "Which Jews will be saved as described by Paul in Romans 11:26?" The answer is, "All the Jews that remain at the end of the Tribulation, which amounts to one-third of their population at the time. God will graciously woo them individually (as to justifying faith) and corporately (as to number) to national salvation."

Treat Unbelieving Jews Like all other Unbelievers

On an individual basis, an unbelieving Jew is just like any other lost sinner. Every person is made in God's image and is thus sacred. Every soul belongs to God (Ezek 18:4). But every person is conceived and born dead in sin (Ps 51:5), separated from God and a child of wrath (Eph 2:3). They need the Savior, so they need to hear the gospel (Rom 10:9-17). Individual Jews should receive no preferential treatment from us because they come from the loins of Abraham, nor should they be subject to undue disdain as though they are the sole "Christ-killers." The apostles set the example for us in the Book of Acts as they simply went out and preached the gospel to all sinners, calling all, Jew and Gentile, to believe and repent. Peter preached the gospel to lost Jews on Pentecost (Acts 2) and preached to lost Gentiles in Caesarea

(Acts 10:24). Paul preached the gospel to all sinners—regardless of race, creed, gender, socio-economic status (Gal 3:28). When possible, as he entered new towns or cities, he first tried to find a synagogue, since he was a rabbi, where he could preach the gospel to the Jews (Acts 17:1-2). Paul said the gospel is for the Jew first and then for non-Jews (Rom 1:16). He was primarily talking about a historical, chronological and practical strategy of evangelism in that verse. After preaching to the Jews he would then preach to the Gentiles, or anyone who would listen (Acts 17:17). So be like Paul. Treat unbelieving Jews as objects of the gospel and as candidates for salvation like any other sinner:

> [19]For though I am free from all *men*, I have made myself a slave to all, so that I may win more. [20]To the Jews I became as a Jew, so that I might win Jews; to those who are under the Law, as under the Law though not being myself under the Law, so that I might win those who are under the Law; [21]to those who are without law, as without law, though not being without the law of God but under the law of Christ, so that I might win those who are without law. [22]To the weak I became weak, that I might win the weak; I have become all things to all men, so that I may by all means save some (1 Cor 9:19-22).

Be Prayerful for the Jews and Israel

Jesus told His followers how to pray as outlined in the famous "Our Father" prayer (Matt 6). Jesus did not intend it to be a *mantra* or some magical incantation to be mindlessly repeated over and over. It was rather a model or pattern of prayer with guiding principles.

Christians think this is a Christian prayer. But remember, Jesus modeled this prayer to Jews who were at the time living in the Old Covenant theocracy of Israel. And Jesus was a Jewish Rabbi under the Mosaic Law. So when Jesus told the

Jewish disciples to pray, "Thy kingdom come, Thy will be done on earth as it is in heaven," that meant something very specific to them. They took this to mean that they should be praying for YHWH to fulfill all the Old Testament promises He gave regarding the earthly kingdom—and it was to be a Jewish kingdom with headquarters in Jerusalem (cf. Acts 1:6). And the nation of Israel will have a central role. As Christians we should be praying for this earthly manifestation of the kingdom. As believers in Christ, we will be privileged to be a part of this future kingdom (Rev 2:26-27; 3:21; 5:10; 20:4-6; cf. Dan 7:14, 18). This is our future and destiny. This reality should influence our prayer life.

As for individual unsaved Jews, we need to be like Paul who specifically prayed for their salvation. Paul was heart-broken over lost Jews:

> I am telling the truth in Christ, I am not lying, my conscience testifies with me in the Holy Spirit, that I have great sorrow and unceasing grief in my heart. For I could wish that I myself were accursed, *separated* from Christ for the sake of my brethren, my kinsmen according to the flesh, who are Israelites, to whom belongs the adoption as sons, and the glory and the covenants and the giving of the Law and the *temple* service and the promises, whose are the fathers, and from whom is the Christ according to the flesh, who is over all, God blessed forever. Amen....my heart's desire and my prayer to God for them is for *their* salvation (Rom 9:1-5; 10:1).

Read and Study the Old Testament Regularly

Our local church has a formal membership and a formal membership process. Formal membership has served our elders and people well. One of the basic questions we ask the prospective members in addition to their testimony is "Have you ever read the whole Old Testament?" We began asking that question after years of shepherding as we realized more and more that many of our sheep did not ever read the Old Testament, and as a result could not appreciate the fullness of the gospel and the New Testament.

The Bible is one unified story. It has a beginning (Genesis) and an end (Revelation). Only reading the New Testament while neglecting the Old is like reading only the last 100 pages of a 500-page novel. The New Testament is the fulfillment of the Old. It directly quotes the Old Testament over 300 times. Jesus taught from the Hebrew Bible. Paul, a Jewish Rabbi, also taught from the Old Testament as a Christian apostle and it was the basis of his New Testament doctrine. The early church, beginning on the Day of Pentecost, was strictly a Jewish church. It is no coincidence that Jesus died on Passover and that the church began on Pentecost (the Feast of weeks). These two festivals were two of the most important feast days for the nation of Israel (cf. Exod 12; 34:22; Lev 23:5; Num 9; Deut 16; Josh 5:10). Sadly, many Christians don't comprehend the great significance that the Israelite feasts of Passover and Pentecost contribute to the meaning of the gospel and Christianity because they neglect the Old Testament. When the church began, believers did not just stop being completely Jewish. The apostles continued to go daily to the Temple for prayer. The earliest Christians actually had church at the Temple of Israel! (cf. Acts 2:46). They continued to go to the synagogues. Paul taught the Old Testament in the synagogues on a regular basis twenty years after Jesus died (Acts 17:1-2). He celebrated Israelite feast days as a Christian apostle. He took a Nazarite vow at the height of his apostolic ministry (Acts 18:18). The Nazarite vow has no meaning apart from the Old Testament (Num 6).

Some foundational New Testament concepts, such as the New Covenant (Luke 22:20; 1 Cor 11:25; 2 Cor 3:6; Heb 8:7), cannot be understood apart from their Old Testament origin and context (i.e., Exod 12; Jer 31; Ezek 36). Entire New Testament books cannot be properly interpreted apart from a thorough understanding of the Old Testament. Revelation is the sequel to the Book of Daniel and it makes over 400 allusions to the Old Testament. Hebrews is the counterpart to Leviticus and the entire Torah.

Jesus Christ our Savior cannot be fully appreciated apart from a thorough study of the Old Testament. He fulfilled over 100 Old Testament prophecies; He is the incarnation of many Old Covenant types. His person and work are the substance of the all-important Old Testament Tabernacle, Temple, the Temple furniture, Temple sacrifices, priesthood and all the vital Israelite feast days. He is the ultimate Davidic King of Israel and the quintessential Prophet of Israel. He is the Great High Priest foreshadowed by all the Old Testament Jewish high priests who came before Him. Why Jesus died (as the Passover Lamb; Isa 53), when He died (on Passover; 1 Cor 5:7), and how He died (on a tree as a curse—Gal 3:13; cf. Deut 21:22-23; Ps 22) are defined and have meaning only in light of the Old Testament (according to the Old Testament Scriptures; 1 Cor 15:3).

The very nature and character of God cannot be fully appreciated apart from knowing the whole Old Testament. The whole Old Testament is the story of YHWH's relationship with His elect Bride (the book of Hosea), the nation of Israel. God's very name is "the God of Abraham, Isaac and Jacob" (1 Kings 18:36), "the God of the Hebrews" (Exod 3:18), and "the God of Israel" (Exod 5:1). The Old Testament is about Israel and the Jews. To ignore that reality is to truncate God's complete story of redemption.

And finally, Christians should regularly read the Old

Testament because God commands the church to do so. Paul tells of the practical benefit Christians gain from reading the Old testament:

> For whatever was written in earlier times was written for our instruction, so that through perseverance and the encouragement of the Scriptures we might have hope (Rom 15:4).

> 6Now these things happened as examples for us, so that we would not crave evil things as they also craved. 7Do not be idolaters, as some of them were; as it is written, "The people sat down to eat and drink, and stood up to play." 8Nor let us act immorally, as some of them did, and twenty-three thousand fell in one day. 9Nor let us try the Lord, as some of them did, and were destroyed by the serpents. 10Nor grumble, as some of them did, and were destroyed by the destroyer. 11Now these things happened to them as an example, and they were written for our instruction, upon whom the ends of the ages have come (1 Cor 10:6-11).

Be Discerning and Selective with Your Study Tools

The Old Testament can be a challenge to understand in light of many factors: it was written in Hebrew and Aramaic; it's in the context of an ancient culture; we are separated from the events that happened by 2,400-plus years, just to name a few. Nevertheless, it's God's book intended for His people and He wants us to understand it (Ps 119:34). As such God gave His people teachers to explain His Word. Ezra was an Old Testament teacher who explained the Scriptures to the people in a way they could easily understand and apply God's Word (Neh 8:6, 8). In the Church era God has given His people pastors and teachers so they can explain God's Word to the saints (Eph 4:11).

For 2,000 years many godly pastors and teachers have written resources to aid the saints in Bible study. Many men of God invested countless hours of toil and labor writing these resources for the sole purpose of wanting to help the saints in their day and in the years to come. As you read and study the Old Testament keep a few reliable resources by your side. You don't need many; you just need a few excellent ones. Here, we need to be discerning and selective. Not all Bible commentaries and study tools were created equal. There are some really bad ones that can lead you far astray. Beware! (1 Thess 5:21).

Let me suggest some personal favorites that I have relied on for over 30 years on the specific issue of Israel, and in particular, Israel's relation to the Church and the future. The two-volume *The Bible Knowledge Commentary* edited by John Walvoord and Roy Zuck is a must. I always go there first, and have since 1987. It's expositional and filled with helpful charts and maps and visual aids. Most importantly, the many contributors abide by a consistent grammatical-historical hermeneutic. As a result, they all end up with a consistent and complimentary ecclesiology, eschatology and Israelology. Next, I recommend *The MacArthur Study Bible*. Pastor John MacArthur was assisted by the faculty of The Master's Seminary in producing this top-rate study Bible. It also is loaded with helpful charts, maps and graphics complemented by insightful brief commentary, and it is spot on with respect to Israel. A recent (2014), excellent one-volume commentary on the whole Bible at the top of the list is *The Moody Bible Commentary*, with contributions from 30 different scholars. Other scholars and commentators who are solid on Israel include Charles Feinberg, Warren Wiersbe, Robert L. Thomas, Arnold Fruchtenbaum, Randall Price, Michael

Vlach,[104] Larry Pettegrew, John D. Hannah, Erwin Lutzer, Darrell Bock, Mitch Glaser, Charles Dyer, Eugene Merrill, Chuck Swindoll, David Jeremiah, Walt Kaiser, Richard Mayhue, William Barrick, and Thomas Ice to name a few.

Books and authors to stay away from when it comes to Israel and eschatology (the doctrine of the future) are many. They include those theologians who hold to preterism, theonomy, amillennialism, postmillennialism, and covenant theology. The common denominator with them all is that they do not apply the grammatical-historical hermeneutic to prophecy about Israel, but rather resort to varying methods of overly symbolic or allegorical interpretation,[105] and as a result end up all over the map in their subjective interpretations. They also all end up in the same place. They "spiritualize" Israel out of existence and supplant her with the Church. This is called "replacement theology" or

---

104 See for example, *Three Views on Israel and the Church: Perspectives on Romans 9-11*, where Vlach critiques modern non-literal, overly typological hermeneutical approaches that undermine a proper view of Israel; ed. Jared Compton and Andrew David Naselli (Grand Rapids, MI: Kregel Academic, 2018). John C. Whitcomb's, *Esther and the Destiny of Israel*, is a helpful little jewel as well; Winona Lake, Indiana: BMH Books, revised edition, 2005.

105 Pettegrew calls it "extensive typological interpretation," "spiritual interpretation," and "Platonic metaphysical dualism" in reference to the early church fathers (*Forsaking Israel*, 35-37). Although Justin Martyr was one of the first to use allegory in reference to Israel and the Old Testament, he did not invent allegorical interpretation. The Greeks did, and then Philo the Jew (d. AD 50) adopted this hermeneutic and popularized it. From him it leaked into the early church by way of the church fathers. For detailed information on Philo's influence see, Bernard Ramm, *Protestant Biblical Interpretation* (Baker Publishing Group, 1950, revised 1999).

"supersessionism." For them, in the end, Israel has no place as promised by God in the Old Testament.[106]

Many of these theologians are solid in other areas—soteriology, theology proper, practical living—but not in eschatology. Some laborious research might be in order here when trying to vet your tools for study of the Old Testament and Israel, but it is definitely worth it.

Summary

In this chapter seven suggestions have been given to guide Christians in cultivating a biblical attitude and paradigm for thinking about Israel and the Jews. This is particularly needed today in light of all the confusion as well as growing sentiment all over the world characterized by hostility toward Israel...even in the church. First, Christians should heed Paul's advice in Romans 9-11 by being humble instead of arrogant and conceited about unbelieving Israel. Second, believers should be like Jesus and have compassion for lost Jews. Third, church saints should remember the Abrahamic Covenant is still in effect and so God will continue to bless friends of Israel and curse their enemies. Fourth, Christians should treat unbelieving Jews like any other sinner who needs to hear the gospel. Fifth, believers need to be in prayer for Israel just like the apostle Paul modeled for the church. Sixth, Christians should regularly be studying and reading the whole Old Testament in order to become deeper in their own faith and more conversant with the whole counsel of God, much of which is about God's special people, Israel. And finally, seventh, believers need to be discerning in Bible study with

---

[106] One of the most popular and influential replacement theologians today in the Evangelical world is N. T. Wright, whose aggressive disregard for Israel's future is actually dangerous.

respect to choosing resources, commentaries and books on the topic of eschatology, ecclesiology and Israel. Proper hermeneutics demands a consistent, literal interpretation after the pattern of the time-honored grammatical-historical approach. Allegorizing or any other method that ignores the historical context or minimizes original intent of the original author in any given passage distorts the clear meaning of God's Word.

Appendix:
Maps of the Promised Land
Through the Ages

Creation began in the Middle East and world history will culminate in the Middle East. And the Promised Land is featured as central to those two paramount realities. In fact, the entire inspired historical drama of the Bible unfolds on the stage of the Promised Land and its surroundings. The boundaries of the Promised Land have morphed and at times have even become obscured throughout history, many times depending on Israel's faithfulness or disobedience or also due, at times, to God's unique plan for a certain season.

The following fifteen maps are designed to help the reader understand the fluid historical movements that had an impact on the Promised Land's seemingly ever-changing boundaries, demographics and constitution over time, beginning with Creation and culminating with the earthly Millennium Kingdom as depicted by the prophet Ezekiel.

Approximate Location of Eden in Genesis 2 c. 4000 BC

The Origin of the Nations c. 2500 BC, Genesis 10

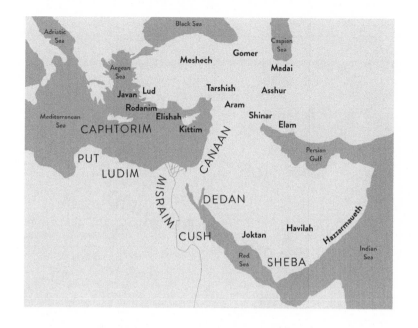

The Land God Promised to Abraham 2100 BC, Genesis 15

The Promised Land Under Joshua 1400 BC

The Promised Land Under David & Solomon 1000 BC

The Divided Kingdom of Israel 931-587 BC

Appendix: Maps of the Promised Land Through the Ages

The Promised Land in Esther 450 BC

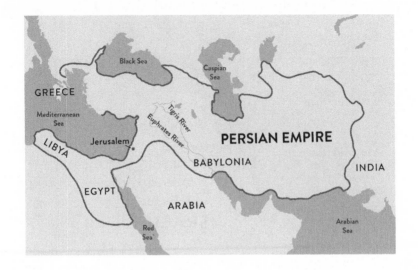

Israel In the Time of Christ

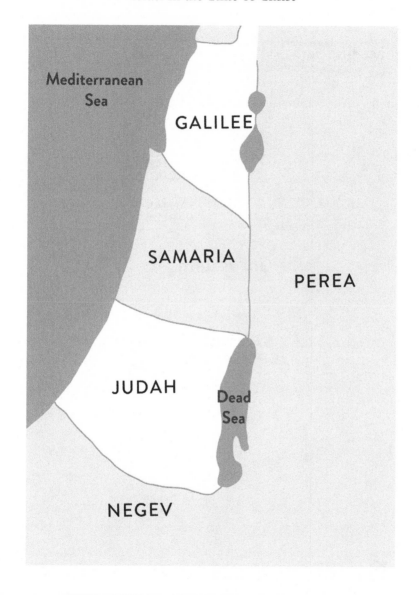

The Promised Land Under Ottoman Rule 1517-1917

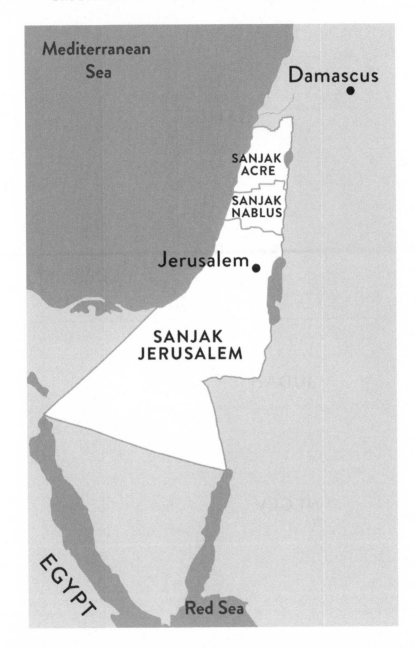

The Promised Land under British Mandate 1923-1948

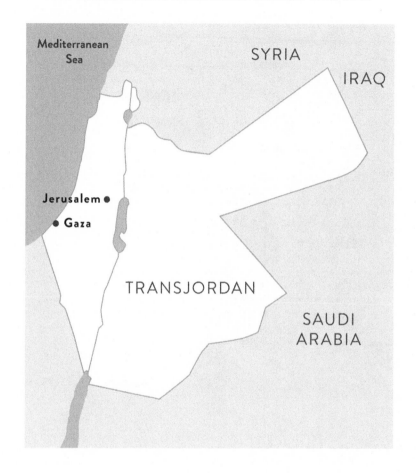

The Promised Land in 1949

The Promised Land 1967

The Promised Land in 2020

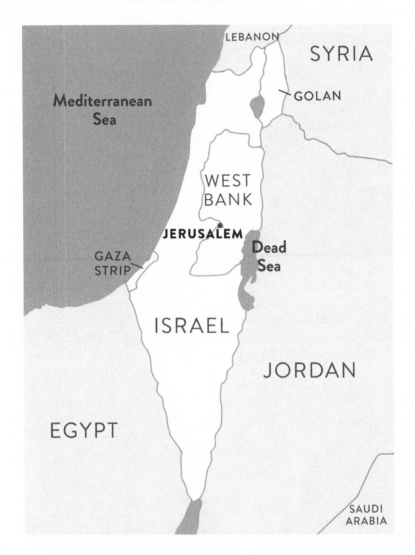

The Promised Land in Ezekiel 38-39 at the end of the age

The Future Promised Land Ezekiel 48

Bibliography

Bock, Darrell and Glaser, Mitch, ed. *Israel, The Church and the Middle East: A Biblical Response to the Current Conflict*. Grand Rapids: Kregel, 2018.

Brog, David. *Reclaiming Israel's History*. Regnery Publishing: Washington, DC, 2017.

Brown, Francis, Driver, S. R. and Briggs, Charles, ed. *The New BDBG Hebrew and English Lexicon with an Appendex Containing the Biblical Aramaic*. Peabody, MA: Hendrickson Publishers, 1979.

Barrick, William. "Inter-covenantal truth and Relevance: Leviticus 26 and the Biblical Covenants," MSJ 21/1 (Spring 2010), 81-102.

Boice, James Montgomery. *The Major Prophets*. Grand Rapids, MI: Kregel Publications, 1986.

Compton, Jared and Naselli, Andrew David, ed. *Three Views on Israel and the Church: Perspectives on Romans 9-11*. Grand Rapids, MI: Kregel Academic, 2018.

Douglas, J. D., ed. *The Illustrated Bible Dictionary: Volume I*. Wheaton, IL: Tyndale House Publishers, 1980.

Douglas, J. D. and Tenney, Merrill C., ed. *The New International Dictionary of the Bible: Pictorial Edition*. Grand Rapids, MI: Zondervan, 1987.

Fast, Howard. *The Jews: A Story of a People*. New York, NY: Dell Publishing, 1968.

Freedman, David Noel, ed. *The Anchor Bible Dictionary*. New York, NY: Doubleday, 1992.

Fruchtenbaum, Arnold G. *Ariel's Bible Commentary: The Book of Genesis*. San Antonio, TX: Ariel Ministries, 2009.

Fruchtenbaum, Arnold. *Israelology: The Missing Link in Systematic Theology*. San Antonio, TX: Ariel Ministries, 1994.

Gaebelein, Frank E., ed. *The Expositor's Bible Commentary*. Grand Rapids, MI: Zondervan, 1986.

Bibliography

Gentry, Kenneth. "The Collapse of the Universe; or the Collapse of Dispensationalism?," *Dispensationalism in Transition* (vol. V, no. 2; February 1992).

Grayzel, Solomon. *A History of the Jews: From the Babylonian Exile to the Present.* The Jewish Publication Society of America, 1968.

Grisanti, Michael A. "The Davidic Covenant," *TMSJ*. 10/2 (Fall 1999), 233-250.

Gritsch, Eric W. Chrsitianhistoryinstitute.org; "Was Luther anti-Semitic?", 1993.

Hoffmeier, James K. *Ancient Israel in Sinai: The Evidence for the Authenticity of the Wilderness Tradition.* New York, NY: Oxford University Press, 2005.

Horner, Barry E. *Eternal Israel: Biblical, Theological, and Historical Studies that Uphold the Eternal, Distinctive Destiny of Israel.* Wordsearch Academic, 2018.

_____. *Future Israel: Why Christian Anti-Judaism Must Be Challenged.* Nashville, TN: B & H Academic, 2007.

Kaiser, Walt. *A History of Israel: From the Bronze Age through the Jewish Wars,* Nashville, TN: B & H Publishers, 1998.

Keil, C. F. and Delitzsch, F. *Commentary on the Old Testament: The Pentateuch.* Peabody, MA: Hendrickson Publishers, 1989.

Kuntzell, Matthias. "National Socialism and Anti-Semitism in the Arab World," *Jewish Political Studies Review,* 17, 1-2 (Spring 2005).

LaHaye, Tim and Ice, Thomas, ed. *The End Times Controversy.* Eugene, OR: Harvest House Publishers, 2003.

Lutzer, Erwin. *Hitler's Cross.* Chicago, IL: Moody Publishers, 1995.

MacArthur, John. *The MacArthur Study Bible: Twentieth-Anniversary Edition,* New King James Version. Nashville, TN: Thomas Nelson, 1997, 2017.

Mathews, Kenneth A. *The New American Commentary: Genesis 1-11:26.* USA: Broadman & Holman Publishers, 1996.

McClintock, John and Strong, James, ed. *Cyclopedia of Biblical, Theological, and Ecclesiastical Literature.* Grand Rapids, MI: Baker Book House, 1981.

Minahan, James. *Encyclopedia of the Stateless Nations.* Westport, CT: Greenwood Press, 2002.

Oberman, Heiko A. *The Roots of Anti-Semitism In the Age of Renaissance and Reformation.* Philadelphia: Fortress Press, 1981, translated from the German by James I. Porter.

Pettegrew, Larry, ed. *Forsaking Israel: How It Happened and Why It Matters.* The Woodlands, TX: Kress Biblical Resources, 2020.

Pettegrew, Larry D. "The New Covenant" 251-270 TMSJ 10/2 (Fall 1999).

Phillips, John. *Exploring Genesis: An Expository Commentary.* Grand Rapids, MI: Kregel Publications, 1980.

Pilkey, John D. *A Mesopotamian Timeline: Volume IV.* Anacortes, WA: R. S. Marshall, 2018.

_____. *A Designed World: The Monogenesis of Man from Noah's Family.* Ross S. Marshall, 2017.

Price, J. Randall. *The Coming Last Days Temple.* Eugene, OR: Harvest House Publishers, 1999.

Price, J. Randall, ed. *What Should We Think about Israel? Separating Fact from Fiction in the Middle East.* Eugene, OR: Harvest House Publishers, 2019.

Ramm, Bernard. *Protestant Biblical Interpretation.* Baker Publishing Group, 1950, revised 1999.

Richardson, Peter. *Israel In the Apostolic Church.* New York: Cambridge University Press, 1969, 2005.

Ross, Allen P. *Creation and Blessing: A Guide to the Study and Exposition of Genesis.* Grand Rapids: Baker Academic, 1998.

Roth, Cecil, ed. *Encyclopedia Judaica, Volumes 1-16.* Jerusalem, Israel: Keter Publishing House, 1971, 1973.

Rydelnik, Michael and Vanlaningham, Michael, ed. *The Moody Bible Commentary.* Chicago, IL: Moody Publishers, 2014.

Sproul, R. C., ed. *The Reformation Study Bible: Condensed Edition, ESV.* Orlando, FL: Reformation Trust Publishing, 2017.

Tenney, Merrill C, ed. *The Zondervan Pictorial Encyclopedia of the Bible.* Grand Rapids, MI: Zondervan, 1976.

Thomas, Robert L. *Revelation 1-7: An Exegetical Commentary.* Chicago: Moody Press, 1992.

Timmerman, Kenneth R. *Preachers of Hate: Islam and the War on America.* New York, NY: Crown Forum, 2003.

Unger, Merrill F. and R. K. Harrison, ed. *The New Unger's Bible Dictionary.* Chicago: Moody Press, 1988.

Van Gemeren, Willem A., ed. *New International Dictionary of Old Testament Theology & Exegesis.* Grand Rapids, MI: General, Zondervan, 1997.

Bibliography

Vlach, Michael J. *He Will Reign Forever: A Biblical Theology of the Kingdom of God.* Silverton, OR: Lampion Press.

Vos, Geerhardus. *The Pauline Eschatology.* Phillipsburg, NJ: Presbyterian and Reformed, rep 1991 [1930].

_____. Biblical Theology: Old and New Testaments. Carlisle, PA: The Banner of Truth Trust, 2000.

Walvoord, John F. *Every Prophecy of the Bible.* Colorado Springs, CO: Chariot Victor Publishing, 1999.

Walvoord, John F. and Roy B. Zuck, ed. *The Bible Knowledge Commentary: Old Testament.* Wheaton, IL: Victor Books, 1988.

Wenham, Gordon J. *Word Biblical Commentary: Genesis 1-15.* Thomas Nelson Publishers: Nashville, 1987.

Whitcomb, John C. *Esther and the Destiny of Israel.* Winona Lake, Indiana: BMH Books, revised edition, 2005.

Wiersbe, Warren. *The Wiersbe Bible Commentary: The Complete OT in One Volume.* Colorado Springs, CO: David C. Cook, 2007.

Wood, Leon J. *A Survey of Israel's History.* Grand Rapids, MI: Zondervan Academic, 1986.

Scripture Index

Scripture Index

Scripture Index

Author Index

Author Index

ABOUT THE AUTHOR

Cliff McManis is an Elder and the teaching-pastor at Creekside Bible Church in Cupertino, CA. He graduated from The Master's University and The Master's Seminary. In addition to shepherding in the local church, he also serves as Associate Professor of Theology training pastors at The Cornerstone Bible College and Seminary in Vallejo. He is the author of several books, including *Apologetics by the Book*, *The Biblically-Driven Church* and *What the Bible Says about Confrontation*. He serves as the General Editor of With All Wisdom Publications. Cliff and his family live in Northern California.

ABOUT WITH ALL WISDOM

With All Wisdom is the book publishing ministry of Creekside Bible Church in Cupertino, CA. We started this publishing ministry out of the simple desire to serve our local body with substantive biblical resources for the sake of our people's growth and spiritual maturity. But we also believe that book publishing, like any other Christian ministry, should first and foremost be under the supervision and accountability of the local church. While we are grateful for and will continue to support the many excellent traditional publishers available today–our shelves are full of the books they have produced–we also believe that the best place to develop solid, life-giving theology and biblical instruction is within the local church.

With All Wisdom is also unique because we offer our books at a very low cost. We strive for excellence in our writing and seek to provide a high-quality product to our readers. Our editorial team is comprised of men and women who are highly trained and excellent in their craft. But since we are able to avoid the high overhead costs that are typically incurred by traditional publishers, we are able to pass significant savings on to you. The result is a growing collection of books that are substantive, readable, and affordable.

In order to best serve various spiritual and theological needs of the body of Christ, we have developed three distinct lines of books. **Big Truth|little books**® provides readers with accessible, manageable works on theology, Christian living, and important church and social issues in a format that is easy to read and easy to finish. Our **Equip Series** is aimed at Christians who desire to delve a little deeper into doctrine and practical matters of the faith. Our **Foundations Series** is our academic line in which we seek to contribute to the contemporary theological discussion by combining pastoral perspective with rigorous scholarship.

OTHER TITLES FROM WITH ALL WISDOM

Please visit us at WithAllWisdom.org
to learn more about these titles

BIG TRUTH little books®

A Biblical View of Trials
Cliff McManis

What the Bible Says About Gray Areas
Cliff McManis

Faith: The Gift of God
Cliff McManis

The Problem of Evil
Cliff McManis

What the Bible Says About Government
Cliff McManis

God Defines and Defends Marriage
Cliff McManis

Protecting the Flock: The Priority of Church Membership
Cliff McManis

Educating Your Child: Public, Private, or Homeschool?
A Biblical Perspective
Cliff McManis

What the Bible Says About Depression
Cliff McManis

What the Bible Says About Confrontation
Cliff McManis

Fellowship with God:
A Guide to Bible Reading, Meditation, and Prayer
Derek Brown

What the Bible Says About Hospitality
Cliff McManis

The Danger of Hypocrisy:
Coming to Grips with Jesus' Most Damning Sermon
J.R. Cuevas

Solomon's Great Commission: A Theology of Earthly Life
Derek Brown